PRIMARY MATHEMATICS

WORKBOOK 5A

Common Core Edition

SINGAPORE MATH® PROGRAM

Marshall Cavendish Education

US Distributor

SM Singapore Math Inc.®

Original edition published under the title Primary Mathematics Workbook 5A
© 1981 Curriculum Planning & Development Division, Ministry of Education, Singapore
Published by Times Media Private Limited

This edition © 2014 Marshall Cavendish Education Pte Ltd
(Formerly known as Marshall Cavendish International (Singapore) Private Limited)

Published by Marshall Cavendish Education
Times Centre, 1 New Industrial Road, Singapore 536196
Customer Service Hotline: (65) 6213 9444
US Office Tel: (1-914) 332 8888 | Fax: (1-914) 332 8882
E-mail: tmesales@mceducation.com
Website: www.mceducation.com

Distributed by
Singapore Math Inc.®
19535 SW 129th Avenue
Tualatin, OR 97062
Tel: (503) 557 8100
Website: www.singaporemath.com

First published 2014

Primary Mathematics Common Core Edition Workbook 5A
ISBN 978-981-01-9849-7

Printed in the United States of America

Primary Mathematics (Common Core Edition) is adapted from Primary Mathematics Workbook 5A (3rd Edition),
originally developed by the Ministry of Education, Singapore. This edition contains new content developed by
Marshall Cavendish Education Pte Ltd, which is not attributable to the Ministry of Education, Singapore.

We would like to acknowledge the contributions by:

The Project Team from the Ministry of Education, Singapore that developed the original Singapore edition
Project Director: Dr Kho Tek Hong
Team Members: Hector Chee Kum Hoong, Liang Hin Hoon, Lim Eng Tann, Ng Siew Lee, Rosalind Lim Hui Cheng,
Ng Hwee Wan

Primary Mathematics (Common Core Edition)
Richard Askey, Emeritus Professor of Mathematics from University of Wisconsin, Madison
Jennifer Kempe, Curriculum Advisor from Singapore Math Inc.®

CONTENTS

EXERCISE 1

1. Write each of the following in words.
   (a) 104,102

   [   ]

   (b) 65,598,000

   [   ]

   (c) 11,011,011,011

   [   ]

   (d) 945,025

   [   ]

   (e) 45,045,200

   [   ]

   (f) 100,100,001

   [   ]

   (g) 123,000,000,123

   [   ]

2. Fill in the boxes.
   (a) 6,000,000 + 50,000 + 4,000 + 10 = [   ]

   (b) 35,200,000,000 + 3,000,000 + 800,000 + 500 = [   ]

   (c) 7,000,000 + [   ] + 2,000 + 5 = 7,852,005

   (d) 36,000,000,000 + [   ] + 700,000 + 50,000
       = 37,000,750,000

3. Write each of the following in standard form.

(a) nine billion, nine million, nine hundred thousand, nine

[   ]

(b) fifteen million, fifteen

[   ]

(c) one million, one thousand, one

[   ]

(d) 45 millions 8 hundreds 9 tens

[   ]

(e) 123 thousands 4 tens 5 ones

[   ]

(f) 1,600 thousands 8 hundreds

[   ]

(g) 4 millions 230 thousands

[   ]

(h) Forty-six billion, four hundred twenty thousand, two

[   ]

4. Find the value of each of the following.

(a) 4 billions is [   ] thousands.

(b) How many hundred thousands are in 4,823,500? [   ]

(c) 62,503,410 is [   ] thousands greater than 3,410.

5. Saturn is about 821,190,000 miles from Earth.

(a) The digit [   ] is in the ten thousands place.

(b) The value of the digit 8 is [   ].

(c) There are [   ] millions in 821,190,000.

(d) There are [   ] thousands in 821,190,000.

6. Find the value of each of the following.

    (a) 45,802,000 is [ ] million more than 802,000.

    (b) There are [ ] millions in 45,802,000.

7. (a) What number is 1 less than ten million? [ ]

    (b) What number is 100 less than ten million? [ ]

    (c) What number is 1,000 less than ten million? [ ]

    (d) What number is 10,000 less than ten million? [ ]

8. Check (✔) the box beside each true statement.

    (a) Three thousand more than 54,013,020 is 54,043,020. [ ]

    (b) Twenty million more than 5,871,800,025 is 5,891,800,025. [ ]

    (c) Fifty thousand less than 10,000,000 is 9,950,000. [ ]

    (d) One hundred thousand less than 123,456,789 is 122,456,789. [ ]

9. Write > or < in each ( ).

    (a) 9,999,999,999 ( ) 10,000,000,000

    (b) 32,586,153 ( ) 8,985,653

    (c) 54,013,020 ( ) forty million, nine hundred thousand, twenty-two

    (d) 358,568,486 ( ) one billion

10. Arrange the numbers in decreasing order.

    560,018,000   65,018,000   560,810,000

    [ ]

Unit 1: Whole Numbers

7

EXERCISE 2

1. Round each number to the nearest ten thousand.

    (a) 10,600

    (b) 234,200

    (c) 459,900

2. Round each number to the nearest hundred thousand.

    (a) 1,585,100

    (b) 15,851,000

    (c) 158,510,000

3. Round each number to the nearest million.

    (a) 8,385,000

    (b) 35,680,800

    (c) 555,555,555

4. Round each number to the nearest ten million.

    (a) 287,185,000

    (b) 652,100,600

    (c) 69,103,301

5. Round each number to the nearest hundred million.

    (a) 180,169,400

    (b) 7,658,588,102

    (c) 51,609,560,005

EXERCISE 3

1. Add.

(a)	2,700,000 + 900,000 =
(b)	800,000 + 500,000 =
(c)	3,200,000 + 800,000 =

2. Subtract.

(a)	5,300,000 − 400,000 =
(b)	600,000 − 200,000 =
(c)	4,500,000 − 600,000 =

3. Multiply.

(a)	80,000 × 2 =
(b)	50,000 × 4 =
(c)	200,000 × 6 =

4. Divide.

(a)	180,000 ÷ 6 =
(b)	240,000 ÷ 8 =
(c)	560,000 ÷ 7 =

5. Estimate the value of each of the following.

(a) 306,481 + 560,423 ≈ 300,000 + 600,000
    =

(b) 483,176 + 820,533 ≈

(c) 2,546,831 + 692,500 ≈

(d) 8,672,390 + 920,767 ≈

(e) 735,601 − 398,842 ≈

(f) 930,652 − 456,841 ≈

(g) 3,654,704 − 886,512 ≈

(h) 6,300,649 − 100,874 ≈

6. Estimate the value of each of the following.

(a) 330,667 × 2 ≈ 300,000 × 2
          =

330,667 ≈ 300,000

(b) 481,192 × 4 ≈

(c) 828,676 × 6 ≈

(d) 956,057 × 5 ≈

(e) 514,689 ÷ 3 ≈ 600,000 ÷ 3
          =

(f) 475,999 ÷ 6 ≈

(g) 526,843 ÷ 5 ≈

(h) 639,813 ÷ 9 ≈

EXERCISE 4

1. Find the factors of each of the following.

(a) 48

$48 = 1 \times 48$ $48 = 2 \times 24$ $48 = 3 \times 16$
$48 = 4 \times 12$ $48 = 6 \times 8$

The factors of 48 are _____.

(b) 72

(c) 128

(d) 150

---

2. What number am I?

(a) I am between 20 and 40.
   I am a multiple of 5.
   I am a factor of 60.

   I am _____.

(b) I am smaller than 80.
   I am a common multiple of 8 and 10.

   I am _____.

(c) I am smaller than 100.
   I am a common multiple of 24 and 36.

   I am _____.

(d) I am the lowest common multiple of 2, 4, and 7.

   I am _____.

3. Find the missing factors.

(a) ☐ × 6 = 84

(b) 5 × ☐ = 120

(c) ☐ × 3 = 99

(d) ☐ × 5 = 75

(e) 4 × ☐ = 116

(f) 6 × ☐ = 132

4. List the first four multiples of each number.

(a) 5

(b) 7

(c) 8

(d) 9

5. Find the lowest common multiple of each set of numbers.

(a) 3 and 5

(b) 6 and 8

(c) 4, 6, and 9

6. Find the greatest common factor for each pair of numbers.

(a) 12 and 72

(b) 18 and 57

(c) 48 and 84

EXERCISE 5

1. List all the prime numbers between 1 and 50.
   Use the number chart below to help you.

1	2	3	4	5	6	7	8	9	10
11	12	13	14	15	16	17	18	19	20
21	22	23	24	25	26	27	28	29	30
31	32	33	34	35	36	37	38	39	40
41	42	43	44	45	46	47	48	49	50

2. List all the prime numbers between 50 and 60.

3. Fill in the boxes with prime numbers.

   (a) $5 \times 4 = 5 \times \boxed{} \times \boxed{}$

   (b) $6 \times 9 = \boxed{} \times 3 \times 3 \times 3$

   (c) $45 \times 2 = \boxed{} \times \boxed{} \times 3 \times 2$

   (d) $14 \times 6 = 2 \times \boxed{} \times 2 \times \boxed{}$

4. List the composite numbers between 47 and 51 and show the prime factorization of each.

EXERCISE 6

1. Rewrite each of the following using exponents.

   (a) 2 × 2 × 3 × 5

   (b) 7 × 11 × 7 × 11 × 2

   (c) 3 × 2 × 3 × 2 × 3

   (d) 7 × 7 × 3 × 3 × 2

   (e) 5 × 5 × 11 × 11 × 11

   (f) 2 × 2 × 13 × 13 × 31 × 2

   (g) 5 × 3 × 19 × 3 × 19 × 5 × 2

2. Find the value of each of the following.

   (a) $2^4 \times 3^3$

   (b) $2^2 \times 7^2$

   (c) $11^2 \times 3^2$

   (d) $10^2 \times 10^3$

3. Write **>**, **<**, or **=** in each ◯.

   (a) 3^4 ◯ 3 × 4   (b) 2^2 ◯ 2 × 2

   (c) 2^3 ◯ 2 × 2 × 2   (d) 4^3 ◯ 3 × 3 × 3 × 3

   (e) 5 × 5 × 5 ◯ 3^5 (f) 7^4 ◯ 49 × 49

   (g) 2^4 ◯ 4^2 (h) $3^2 \times 2^3$ ◯ 9 × 8

Unit 1: Whole Numbers

4. Rewrite the following as powers of 10.
   (a) 10,000

   (b) 1,000,000

   (c) 1 billion

5. Find the value of each of the following.
   (a) $2 \times 10 \times 10 \times 10$

   (b) 8×10^5

   (c) 62×10^7

6. Express each of the following as a product of prime factors using exponents.
   (a) 28

   (b) 54

   (c) 88

   (d) 108

7. Express each of the following as a product of prime factors using exponents.
   (a) 10^2

   (b) 10^3

   (c) 10^4

   (d) 10^5

   (e) 10^{100}

EXERCISE 7

1. Multiply.

   (a) $238 \times 10 =$ [ ]

   (b) $10 \times 400 =$ [ ]

   (c) $700 \times 100 =$ [ ]

   (d) $100 \times 280 =$ [ ]

   (e) $37 \times 1,000 =$ [ ]

   (f) $1,000 \times 520 =$ [ ]

2. Multiply 56 by 7. $56 \times 7 =$ [ ]

   Then fill in the boxes.

   (a) $56 \times 70 =$ [ ]

   (b) $56 \times 700 =$ [ ]

   (c) $56 \times 7,000 =$ [ ]

3. Multiply 75 by 9. $75 \times 9 =$ [ ]

   Then fill in the boxes.

   (a) $75 \times 90 =$ [ ]

   (b) $75 \times 900 =$ [ ]

   (c) $75 \times 9,000 =$ [ ]

4. Multiply.

(a) 254 × 10 =	(b) 602 × 100 =
(c) 93 × 40 =	(d) 57 × 1,000 =
(e) 43 × 600 =	(f) 392 × 800 =
(g) 728 × 5,000 =	(h) 8,056 × 3,000 =

5. Estimate the value of each of the following.

(a) $326 \times 47 \approx 300 \times 50$ $\qquad\qquad\qquad =$
(b) $78 \times 586 \approx$
(c) $32 \times 705 \approx$
(d) $4{,}165 \times 53 \approx$

6. Andrew wants to buy 28 radio sets. Each radio set costs $229. Give a quick estimate of the total cost of the radio sets.

7. Give a quick estimate of the area of a rectangle with length 114 in. and width 92 in.

EXERCISE 8

1. Divide 72 by 8. $72 \div 8 =$ ▭

    Then fill in the boxes.

    (a) $720,000 \div 80 =$ ▭

    (b) $720,000 \div 800 =$ ▭

    (c) $720,000 \div 8,000 =$ ▭

2. Divide 900 by 6. $900 \div 6 =$ ▭

    Then fill in the boxes.

    (a) $90,000 \div 60 =$ ▭

    (b) $90,000 \div 600 =$ ▭

    (c) $90,000 \div 6,000 =$ ▭

3. Divide.

(a) $360 \div 10 =$	(b) $4,200 \div 100 =$
(c) $250 \div 50 =$	(d) $5,600 \div 800 =$

4. Divide.

(a) $360 \div 90 =$	(b) $4,080 \div 80 =$
(c) $1,050 \div 70 =$	(d) $60,000 \div 400 =$
(e) $35,000,000 \div 500 =$	(f) $41,200,000 \div 4,000 =$
(g) $630,000 \div 9,000 =$	(h) $960,000 \div 6,000 =$

5. Estimate the value of each of the following.

(a) $282 \div 52 \approx 300 \div 50$
$ =$

(b) $324 \div 42 \approx$

(c) $4{,}406 \div 49 \approx$

(d) $1{,}705 \div 31 \approx$

6. Albert bought 28 DVDs for $805. Give a quick estimate of the cost of each DVD.

7. The floor area of a hall is 1,044 m². The length is 36 m. Give a quick estimate of the width of the hall.

8. There are 426 people attending a conference. The cost per person for a catered lunch is $38.75. Give an estimate of the cost to serve all the people at the conference.

---

9. A zoo wants to estimate how much it would cost to ship some hippos to a new location. An adult hippo weighs an average of 5,710 lbs. The zoo has 6 full-grown hippos and 2 half-grown hippos.

   (a) Estimate the total weight of these hippos.

   (b) If shipping costs 53 ¢ per pound, estimate how much it will cost to ship the hippos.

---

10. A teacher has $4,300 to spend on new computers. Each computer costs $799. Estimate the number of computers the school can buy.

REVIEW 1

1. Write each of the following in words.

   (a) 15,508,000

   [   ]

   (b) 376,920,000

   [   ]

2. Write each of the following in figures.

   (a) sixty billion, eleven   [   ]

   (b) twelve million, nine hundred four thousand   [   ]

   (c) 60 millions   [   ]

   (d) 5 billions 605 thousands   [   ]

3. Write 3,495,002,091 in expanded form.

   [   ]

4. Fill in the boxes.

   (a) In 8,453,000, the digit [   ] is in the hundred
       thousands place.

   (b) In 5,236,000, the digit 3 stands for 3 × [   ].

   (c) The value of digit 8 in 4,781,062,593 is [   ].

   (d) There are [   ] thousands in 418,630,000.

5. Arrange the numbers in decreasing order.

64,013,420   64,013,020   84,043,020   84,403,020

┌───┐
│   │
└───┘

6. Find the value of each of the following.

   (a) 500,000 + 80,000 + 300

   (b) 60,000,000 + 420,000 + 5,000

7. Find the value of each of the following.

   (a) 8,206,000 is 1,000,000 more than ____.

   (b) 62,440,000 is 1,000,000 less than ____.

   (c) 9,345,000 is ____ more than 9,305,000.

   (d) 7,188,000 is ____ less than 7,988,000.

8. Find the value of each of the following.

   (a) Round 49,501 to the nearest hundred.

   (b) Round 49,501 to the nearest thousand.

   (c) Round 3,090,456 to the nearest 100,000.

9. What is the missing number in each box?

   (a) 67 × ____ = 67,000

   (b) ____ × 3,040 = 30,400

   (c) 50,800 ÷ ____ = 508

   (d) 76,000 ÷ ____ = 7,600

10. Estimate the value of each of the following.

(a) 9,869 × 899

(b) 37,496 ÷ 603

11. Write >, <, or = in each ◯.

(a) 33,856,000 − 1,000,000 ◯ 30,856,000

(b) 37,000 + 8,000 ◯ 50,000 − 4,000

(c) 80,000 × 3 ◯ 60 × 400

(d) 400 × 50 ◯ 10,000,000 ÷ 500

(e) 65,000,000 ÷ 1,000 ◯ 650,000

(f) 8,000 + 50 ◯ 8,000 − 100

(g) 450 ÷ 2 ◯ 45 × 2

(h) 64 ◯ 2^8

12. (a) Write the first twelve multiples of 6.

(b) Which one of the following numbers is a
    common multiple of 4, 5, and 10?

    4, 5, 50, 100

(c) Give the first two common multiples of 8 and 9.

13. Find the lowest common multiple of 6 and 10.

14. (a) List all the factors of 100.

(b) Which one of the following numbers has 4 as its factor?

18,   34,   38,   64

15. (a) Which one of the following numbers is a common factor of 45 and 144?

4,   5,   9,   45

(b) Find the common factors of 18 and 24.

(c) Find the greatest common factor of 28 and 84.

16. (a) Find the prime factorization of 58.

(b) Find the prime factorization of 154.

17. Express the following using exponents.

(a) $3 \times 3 \times 2 \times 2 \times 5$

(b) $11 \times 7 \times 13 \times 7 \times 11$

(c) $2 \times 3 \times 11 \times 3 \times 19 \times 19$

18. Express the following as a product of prime factors using exponents.

(a) 333

(b) 60

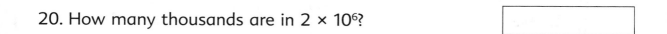

19. Find the value of $6 \times 10^7 + 4 \times 10^5 + 2 \times 10^4 + 5 \times 10^3$.

20. How many thousands are in 2×10^6?

21. Find the value of each of the following.
    (a) 6×10^3

    (b) 42×10^4

    (c) 99×10^5

    (d) 510×10^3

22. Melissa packed 1,830 books into 48 boxes.
    Give a quick estimate of the number of books packed in each box.

23. Jason bought 48 tablets. Each tablet cost $599. Give a quick estimate of the total cost of the tablets.

EXERCISE 1

1. Fill in the boxes.

    (a) $60 + 21 + 40 + 19 =$ ⬚

    (b) $18 + 27 + 22 + 10 =$ ⬚

    (c) $25 \times 18 \times 4 =$ ⬚

    (d) $150 \times 7 \times 5 \times 2 =$ ⬚

2. Check (✔) the box beside each true statement.

    (a) $8 + 9 + 12 + 10 = 10 + 12 + 9 + 8$ ⬚

    (b) $6 \times 9 \times 11 = 9 \times 11 \times 6$ ⬚

    (c) $9 \times 5 + 3 = 9 + 5 \times 3$ ⬚

    (d) $6 + 8 + 2 \times 10 = 6 + 8 \times 10 + 2$ ⬚

3. Find the value of each of the following.

    (a) $31 + 29 + 32 + 28$ ⬚

    (b) $194 + 31 + 9 + 8$ ⬚

    (c) $5 + 43 + 3 + 57 + 8 + 2$ ⬚

    (d) $500 \times 7 \times 2 \times 30$ ⬚

    (e) $150 \times 4 \times 2 \times 30$ ⬚

4. Write a single expression for the following situation. Then solve the expression.

The cost of going to a musical is $12 for adults and $8 for children under 18. A class of 20 fifth graders, along with one teacher and two parent helpers, are going to the musical. There is a $20 discount for a group of at least 10 people. What will be the total cost?

5. Find the value of each of the following.

(a) $138 + (20 - 15)$

(b) $138 + 20 - 15$

(c) $138 - 20 + 15$

(d) $(138 - 20) + 15$

(e) $(64 \div 8) \div 2$

(f) $64 \div (8 \div 2)$

(g) $64 \div 8 \div 2$

(h) $99 \div 3 \times 3$

(i) $(99 \div 3) \times 3$

6. Find the value of each of the following.

(a) $7 \times 9 + 1 \div 1 - 6 \times 3$

(b) $(108 + 12) \div 5 \times 6$

(c) $60 \div 5 + 24$

(d) $20 - 36 \div 6 + 4$ ☐

(e) $49 \div 7 \div 7$ ☐

(f) $(20 - 16) \times (9 - 2)$ ☐

(g) $56 - 8 \times 6$ ☐

(h) $45 - 9 \div 3$ ☐

(i) $300 \div (8 + 2) \times 10$ ☐

(j) $92 - 3 \times [42 - 2 \times (13 - 6)] \div 2$ ☐

(k) $\{26 + [(16 - 4) \div (4 + 2)]\} \times 3$ ☐

7. Write **+**, **−**, **×**, **÷**, or **parentheses** in each ◯ to make each of the following true.

(a) $(\,3\,+\,3\,)\,\div\,3\,-\,3\,\div\,3 = 1$

(b) $3\,◯\,3\,◯\,◯\,3\,◯\,3\,◯\,◯\,3 = 2$

(c) $◯\,3\,◯\,3\,◯\,◯\,3\,◯\,3\,◯\,3 = 3$

(d) $◯\,3\,◯\,3\,◯\,3\,◯\,3\,◯\,◯\,3 = 4$

(e) $3\,◯\,3\,◯\,3\,◯\,3\,◯\,3 = 5$

(f) $◯\,3\,◯\,3\,◯\,3\,◯\,◯\,3\,◯\,3 = 6$

(g) $3\,◯\,3\,◯\,3\,◯\,3\,◯\,3 = 7$

(h) $3\,◯\,3\,◯\,3\,◯\,3\,◯\,3 = 8$

(i) $3\,◯\,3\,◯\,3\,◯\,3\,◯\,3 = 9$

(j) $◯\,3\,◯\,3\,◯\,3\,◯\,◯\,3\,◯\,3 = 10$

EXERCISE 2

1. Check (✔) the box beside each true statement.

    (a) $(8 - 3) \times 5 = (8 \times 5) - (3 \times 5)$ ☐

    (b) $(8 - 3) \times 5 = (8 \times 3) - (5 \times 3)$ ☐

    (c) $(7 + 6) \times 9 = (7 + 9) \times (6 + 9)$ ☐

    (d) $(7 + 6) \times 9 = (7 \times 9) + (6 \times 9)$ ☐

2. Select one true statement from Problem 1.
    Show why it is true with a model.

3. Fill in the missing numbers.

(a) $(77 + 6) \times 7 = (77 \times \boxed{}) + (6 \times \boxed{})$

(b) $(15 + 9) \times 9 = (15 \times \boxed{}) + (9 \times \boxed{})$

(c) $6 \times (21 - 16) = (6 \times \boxed{}) - (6 \times \boxed{})$

(d) $9 \times (12 - 7) = (9 \times 12) - (9 \times \boxed{})$

(e) $(8 \times 5) + (8 \times 4) = 8 \times (5 + \boxed{})$

(f) $(28 - 3) \times 7 = (\boxed{} \times 7) - (3 \times \boxed{})$

(g) $(2 \times 9) + (10 \times 9) = (\boxed{} + \boxed{}) \times 9$

4. Fill in the missing numbers.

(a) $14 \times (3 + 6) = (14 \times 3) + (14 \times \boxed{})$

(b) $20 \times (100 - 15) = (\boxed{} \times 100) - (\boxed{} \times 15)$

(c) $(\boxed{} + 6) \times 5 = (3 \times 5) + (6 \times 5)$

(d) $(52 - \boxed{}) \times 10 = (52 \times \boxed{}) - (2 \times 10)$

(e) $26 \times 11 = (30 \times \boxed{}) - (\boxed{} \times 11)$

(f) $104 \times 12 = (100 \times \boxed{}) + (\boxed{} \times 12)$

(g) $98 \times 7 = (100 \times \boxed{}) - (\boxed{} \times 7)$

(h) $9,998 \times 8 = (10,000 \times \boxed{}) - (\boxed{} \times 8)$

EXERCISE 3

1. Add.

(a) 399 + 54 =

399 + 54 = 400 + 54 − 1

(b) 1,467 + 299 =

(c) 201 + 679 =

1 + 79

(d) 2,043 + 207 =

(e) 520 + 380 =

20 + 80

(f) 1,563 + 437 =

563 + 437

(g) 2,432 + 368 =

(h) 3,254 + 746 =

2. Subtract.

(a) 312 − 99 =

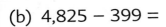

(b) 4,825 − 399 =

(c) 700 − 87 =

(d) 1,200 − 45 =

(e) 3,600 − 589 =

(f) 5,460 − 56 =

(g) 4,000 − 786 =

(h) 5,000 − 85 =

Unit 2: More Calculations with Whole Numbers

3. Add or subtract.

(a) 499 + 307 =

(b) 732 − 99 =

(c) 201 + 359 =

(d) 443 − 299 =

(e) 599 + 472 =

(f) 235 + 470 =

(g) 500 − 73 =

(h) 363 + 507 =

EXERCISE 4

1. Multiply.

(a) 52 × 41 =

52 × 41 = 52 × 40 + 52

(b) 46 × 51 =

(c) 75 × 21 =

(d) 28 × 81 =

(e) 62 × 99 =

62 × 99 = 62 × 100 − 62

(f) 34 × 99 =

(g) 99 × 65 =

(h) 99 × 47 =

Unit 2: More Calculations with Whole Numbers

2. Multiply.

(a) 26 × 49 =

26 × 49 = 26 × 50 − 26

(b) 88 × 29 =

(c) 59 × 36 =

(d) 79 × 54 =

(e) 25 × 32 =

25 × 32 = 25 × 4 × 8

(f) 25 × 80 =

(g) 56 × 25 =

(h) 88 × 25 =

3. Multiply.

(a) 45 × 19 =

(b) 32 × 49 =

(c) 47 × 51 =

(d) 61 × 61 =

(e) 91 × 11 =

(f) 34 × 99 =

(g) 56 × 99 =

(h) 68 × 99 =

Unit 2: More Calculations with Whole Numbers

4. Write an equation for each of the following word problems. Solve using mental math.

   (a) There were 21 trays in a bakery. Each tray held 15 donuts. How many donuts were there altogether?

   (b) A farmer packed 32 plums in each box. There were 98 boxes. How many plums were there in all the boxes?

EXERCISE 5

1. Fill in the missing numbers.

(a) 2,482 + _____ = 3,417

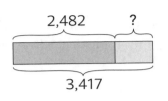

(b) _____ + 783 = 6,004

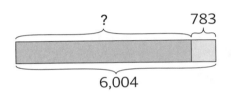

(c) 1,058 − _____ = 469

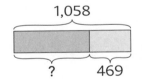

(d) _____ − 472 = 2,983

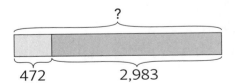

Unit 2: More Calculations with Whole Numbers

2. Fill in the missing numbers.

(a) 4 × _____ = 616

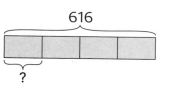

(b) _____ × 7 = 1,435

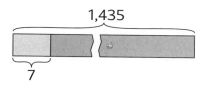

(c) _____ ÷ 5 = 204

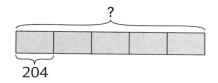

(d) 333 ÷ _____ = 9

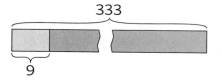

3. At a carnival, Ann sold 314 bottles of drinks a day.
    She sold 66 bottles more in the afternoon than in the morning.
    How many bottles of drinks did she sell in the morning?

---

4. Adele bought a pen. She also bought a book that cost 3 times as
    much as the pen. She spent $112 altogether. Find the cost of the book.

EXERCISE 6

1. Elaine has 274 beads. Of them, 150 are blue, 70 are red, and the rest are white. How many more red beads than white beads are there?

2. Tickets to a concert cost $15 per adult and $8 per child. Nicole bought tickets for 4 adults and 5 children. How much did she spend altogether?

3. Chris paid $36 for 3 similar tank tops and 2 similar T-shirts.
   A T-shirt cost 3 times as much as a tank top.
   How much did Chris pay for 2 T-shirts?

---

4. Peter bought 45 greeting cards at 3 for $2.
   He sold all of them at 5 for $4.
   How much money did he earn?

5. A box of cookies cost $6 and a bottle of milk cost $2. After paying for 2 boxes of cookies and 6 bottles of milk, Matthew had $30 left. How much money did he have at first?

6. Lily and Sara each had an equal amount of money at first. After Lily spent $18 and Sara spent $25, Lily had twice as much as Sara. How much money did each of them have at first?

EXERCISE 7

1. Multiply.

(a) 78 × 40 = $\begin{array}{r} 78 \\ \times\ 40 \\ \hline \end{array}$	(b) 46 × 50 =
(c) 53 × 24 =	(d) 65 × 89 =
(e) 246 × 70 =	(f) 309 × 60 =
(g) 508 × 32 =	(h) 760 × 87 =

Unit 2: More Calculations with Whole Numbers

2. Multiply.

(a) $1{,}257 \times 30 =$ $\begin{array}{r} 1{,}2\,5\,7 \\ \times\qquad 3\,0 \\ \hline \end{array}$	(b) $4{,}008 \times 70 =$
(c) $1{,}870 \times 20 =$	(d) $6{,}229 \times 13 =$
(e) $3{,}424 \times 25 =$	(f) $1{,}003 \times 63 =$
(g) $1{,}075 \times 73 =$	(h) $8{,}207 \times 46 =$

Unit 2: More Calculations with Whole Numbers

3. There are 505 pages in a book. Sara reads 23 pages of the book daily for 17 days. How many more pages does she have to read to finish the whole book?

---

4. A company paid for its employees and families to attend a private concert. The concert was attended by 1,038 people. Half of them were children. The tickets cost $15 for adults and $6 for children. How much did the company pay for the concert?

EXERCISE 8

1. Divide.

(a) $60 \div 20 =$ $20\overline{)60}$	(b) $94 \div 30 =$
(c) $790 \div 80 =$	(d) $577 \div 90 =$
(e) $98 \div 32 =$	(f) $88 \div 49 =$
(g) $580 \div 64 =$	(h) $299 \div 53 =$

EXERCISE 9

1. Divide.

(a) $92 \div 17 =$ $17\overline{)92}$	(b) $85 \div 22 =$
(c) $80 \div 26 =$	(d) $96 \div 34 =$
(e) $361 \div 62 =$	(f) $397 \div 47 =$
(g) $425 \div 54 =$	(h) $192 \div 38 =$

EXERCISE 10

1. Divide.

(a) $528 \div 30 =$ $30\overline{)528}$	(b) $820 \div 40 =$
(c) $307 \div 20 =$	(d) $650 \div 50 =$
(e) $485 \div 15 =$	(f) $700 \div 21 =$
(g) $820 \div 42 =$	(h) $908 \div 56 =$

EXERCISE 11

1. Divide.

(a) $9,963 \div 41 =$ $41\overline{)9,963}$	(b) $8,282 \div 16 =$
(c) $6,600 \div 55 =$	(d) $9,229 \div 29 =$
(e) $2,624 \div 32 =$	(f) $5,821 \div 63 =$
(g) $7,801 \div 48 =$	(h) $3,008 \div 25 =$

2. There were 2,646 guppies. They were put in equal number in 27 tanks. How many guppies were there in each tank?

3. A farmer had 1,088 peaches. She packed them in boxes of 25.

   (a) How many peaches were left unpacked?

   (b) She sold 21 boxes at $9 each. How much did she receive?

REVIEW 2

1. What number must be added to 634 to give the answer 1,000?

2. Find the value of each of the following.

    (a) $120 - 20 \div 5$

    (b) $6 \times 2 + 8 \div 2 \times 4$

    (c) $(15 + 3) \div 5 \times 5$

    (d) $120 \div 12 + 7 \times 8$

    (e) $27 + 96 \div 12 \div 4$

    (f) $(45 + 27) \div (17 - 8)$

    (g) $130 + 50 + 20 + 70 + 50$

    (h) $145 - 25 \times 4$

    (i) $228 \div 6 \times 2$

    (j) $4 - [7 \div (4 + 3) \times 3]$

    (k) $[(87 + 9) \div 3 \div 4 + 2] \times (10 - 5)$

    (l) $240 + 60 \times [5 \div (6 + 18 - 19)]$

    (m) $7 \times (28 - (8 + ((120 - 20) \div 5)))$

3. Write >, <, or = in each .

    (a) $45,800 \times 3 \bigcirc (45,000 \times 3) + (800 \times 3)$

    (b) $250 + (100 - 50) \bigcirc 1,000 \div (8 \div 2)$

4. Fill in the missing number.

$42 \times 23 = (40 \times 23) + (2 \times \boxed{})$

5. What is the missing number in each box?

(a) $56{,}074 - \boxed{} = 52{,}074$

(b) $16 \times 125 = 125 \times 2 \times \boxed{}$

(c) $28 \times 25 = 100 \times \boxed{}$

(d) $999 + 998 = 2{,}000 - \boxed{}$

6. (a) Find the sum of 12,099 and 900. $\boxed{}$

(b) Find the difference between 79 and 2,100. $\boxed{}$

(c) Find the product of 540 and 28. $\boxed{}$

(d) Find the quotient and remainder when 127 is divided by 40. $\boxed{}$

7. There were 200 participants in a concert. There were 4 times as many girls as boys.

(a) How many girls were there? $\boxed{}$

(b) How many more girls than boys were there? $\boxed{}$

8. If 5 pears cost $3, find the cost of 20 pears. $\boxed{}$

9. Lynn ordered a table that cost $150 and 4 chairs that cost $24 each. She paid a deposit of $50. How much did she have to pay when the table and chairs were delivered? $\boxed{}$

10. Robert packed 1,320 stickers into packets of 22 each. He sold all the stickers at $2 per packet. How much money did he make?

11. Lihua bought 5 packets of white envelopes and 3 packets of brown envelopes. There were 112 envelopes in each packet. How many envelopes did she buy altogether?

12. Out of 1,024 people in a theater, 425 are men, 480 are women, and the rest are children. How many more adults than children are there?

13. Mr. Karlson bought 6,582 lb of rice. He packed the rice in bags of 12 lb each. How many bags of rice did he have? How many pounds of rice were left over?

14. String A is 30 cm longer than String B. String B is 60 cm longer than String C. The total length of the three strings is 3 m. Find the length of String C.

15. Miguel had 45 melons. He sold 25 of them at $6 each and sold the rest at $4 each. How much money did he receive?

16. Ashley bought a bed for $295. She also bought 2 mattresses at $65 each. She gave the cashier a $500 note. How much change did she receive?

17. Brandy has 278 stamps. Jane has 64 stamps more than Brandy. Sam and Jane have 500 stamps altogether. How many stamps does Sam have?

---

18. Mr. Peters baked 156 fruit pies for a fair. He sold them in boxes containing 12 fruit pies each. Each box cost $18. How much money did he collect?

19. David and Peter had $90 and $200, respectively. They were each given an equal amount of money. Then Peter had twice as much money as David. How much money did each boy receive?

20. William sold 5 oven toasters and 3 rice cookers for $500. If a rice cooker cost $20 less than an oven toaster, find the cost of a rice cooker.

EXERCISE 1

1. Fill in the missing numerator or denominator in each of the following.

(a) $\dfrac{4}{5} = \dfrac{12}{\Box}$

(b) $\dfrac{3}{7} = \dfrac{\Box}{28}$

(c) $\dfrac{25}{\Box} = \dfrac{5}{8}$

(d) $\dfrac{6}{9} = \dfrac{2}{\Box}$

(e) $\dfrac{2}{12} = \dfrac{\Box}{6}$

(f) $\dfrac{5}{\Box} = \dfrac{10}{12}$

2. Express each of the following as an improper fraction.

(a) $1\frac{2}{3} =$	(b) $1\frac{5}{7} =$
(c) $2\frac{1}{4} =$	(d) $2\frac{3}{8} =$
(e) $3\frac{1}{6} =$	(f) $2\frac{4}{9} =$
(g) $2\frac{9}{10} =$	(h) $3\frac{5}{12} =$

3. Express each of the following as a whole number or a mixed number in its simplest form.

(a) $\frac{14}{3} =$	(b) $\frac{22}{4} =$
(c) $\frac{15}{6} =$	(d) $\frac{30}{5} =$
(e) $\frac{21}{7} =$	(f) $\frac{20}{8} =$
(g) $\frac{17}{10} =$	(h) $\frac{26}{12} =$

4. Write >, <, or = in each $\bigcirc$.

(a) $1\frac{1}{12}$ $\bigcirc$ $1\frac{9}{10}$

(b) $2\frac{3}{10}$ $\bigcirc$ $2\frac{1}{2}$

(c) $\frac{27}{9}$ $\bigcirc$ 3

(d) 2 $\bigcirc$ $1\frac{11}{12}$

(e) $3\frac{4}{5}$ $\bigcirc$ $\frac{38}{10}$

(f) $\frac{25}{8}$ $\bigcirc$ $3\frac{1}{9}$

5. (a) Arrange the numbers in increasing order.

$\frac{13}{3}$, $3\frac{3}{9}$, 4, $3\frac{1}{2}$, $\frac{9}{2}$

(b) Arrange the numbers in decreasing order.

$3\frac{1}{12}$, $5\frac{1}{3}$, 6, $\frac{15}{3}$, $4\frac{9}{10}$

EXERCISE 2

1. Change each improper fraction to a mixed number by division.

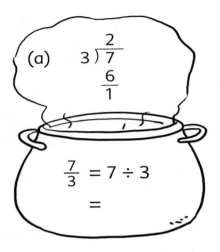

(a)
$$3\overline{)7}$$
with $\frac{2}{7}$, $\frac{6}{1}$

$$\frac{7}{3} = 7 \div 3$$
$$=$$

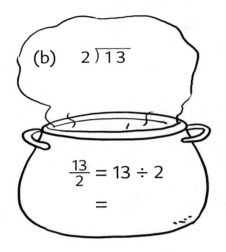

(b)
$$2\overline{)13}$$

$$\frac{13}{2} = 13 \div 2$$
$$=$$

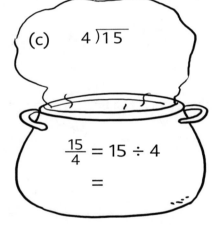

(c)
$$4\overline{)15}$$

$$\frac{15}{4} = 15 \div 4$$
$$=$$

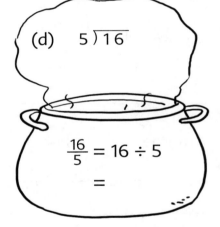

(d)
$$5\overline{)16}$$

$$\frac{16}{5} = 16 \div 5$$
$$=$$

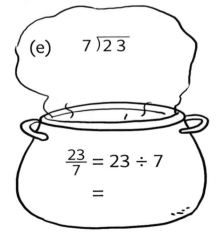

(e)
$$7\overline{)23}$$

$$\frac{23}{7} = 23 \div 7$$
$$=$$

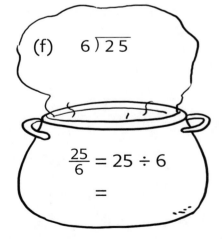

(f)
$$6\overline{)25}$$

$$\frac{25}{6} = 25 \div 6$$
$$=$$

2. Express each improper fraction as a whole number or a mixed number.

(a) $\frac{18}{3} = 18 \div 3 =$ 3$\overline{)18}$	(b) $\frac{19}{5} = 19 \div 5 =$ 5$\overline{)19}$
(c) $\frac{27}{8} =$	(d) $\frac{36}{4} =$

3. Express each of the following answers as a mixed number in its simplest form.

(a) $30 \div 8 =$	(b) $21 \div 4 =$
(c) $35 \div 10 =$	(d) $78 \div 7 =$

4. Larry cut a ribbon into 8 equal pieces. If the ribbon was 26 m long, how many meters long was each piece?

5. Peter poured 2 L of milk equally into 5 jugs. How much milk was there in each jug?

EXERCISE 3

1. Add. Write each answer in its simplest form.

(a) $\dfrac{7}{8} + \dfrac{3}{4} = \dfrac{7}{8} + \dfrac{\square}{8}$

$=$

(b) $\dfrac{2}{3} + \dfrac{4}{9} = \dfrac{\square}{9} + \dfrac{4}{9}$

$=$

(c) $\dfrac{4}{5} + \dfrac{3}{10} =$

(d) $\dfrac{3}{4} + \dfrac{7}{12} =$

(e) $\dfrac{5}{6} + \dfrac{2}{3} =$

(f) $\dfrac{1}{2} + \dfrac{9}{10} =$

2. Add. Write each answer in its simplest form.

(a) $\frac{1}{6} + \frac{3}{4} =$	(b) $\frac{5}{9} + \frac{1}{2} =$
(c) $\frac{1}{2} + \frac{3}{5} =$	(d) $\frac{2}{5} + \frac{3}{4} =$
(e) $\frac{9}{10} + \frac{1}{6} =$	(f) $\frac{3}{10} + \frac{5}{6} =$

EXERCISE 4

1. Subtract. Write each answer in its simplest form.

(a) $\dfrac{7}{8} - \dfrac{3}{4} = \dfrac{7}{8} - \dfrac{\square}{8}$ $=$	(b) $\dfrac{5}{6} - \dfrac{1}{12} = \dfrac{\square}{12} - \dfrac{1}{12}$ $=$
(c) $\dfrac{9}{10} - \dfrac{1}{2} =$	(d) $\dfrac{11}{12} - \dfrac{2}{3} =$
(e) $1\dfrac{1}{2} - \dfrac{3}{4} =$	(f) $1\dfrac{1}{10} - \dfrac{3}{5} =$

2. Subtract. Write each answer in its simplest form.

(a) $\frac{1}{2} - \frac{1}{5} =$

(b) $\frac{7}{12} - \frac{3}{8} =$

(c) $\frac{3}{4} - \frac{3}{10} =$

(d) $\frac{9}{10} - \frac{3}{4} =$

(e) $1\frac{1}{5} - \frac{2}{3} =$

(f) $1\frac{1}{10} - \frac{1}{6} =$

EXERCISE 5

1. Add. Write each answer in its simplest form.

(a) $2\frac{3}{4} + 1\frac{1}{8} = 3\frac{3}{4} + \frac{1}{8}$

$\qquad = 3\frac{\square}{8} + \frac{1}{8}$

$\qquad =$

(b) $1\frac{5}{12} + 3\frac{1}{3} = 4\frac{5}{12} + \frac{1}{3}$

$\qquad = 4\frac{5}{12} + \frac{\square}{12}$

$\qquad =$

(c) $3\frac{7}{10} + 2\frac{2}{5} =$

(d) $2\frac{2}{3} + 2\frac{5}{12} =$

(e) $3\frac{7}{12} + 1\frac{3}{4} =$

(f) $1\frac{4}{5} + 2\frac{7}{10} =$

2. Add. Write each answer in its simplest form.

(a) $2\frac{1}{5} + 1\frac{2}{3} = 3\frac{1}{5} + \frac{2}{3}$

$= 3\frac{\square}{15} + \frac{\square}{15}$

$=$

(b) $2\frac{3}{8} + 2\frac{1}{6} = 4\frac{3}{8} + \frac{1}{6}$

$= 4\frac{\square}{24} + \frac{\square}{24}$

$=$

(c) $1\frac{2}{5} + 5\frac{3}{4} =$

(d) $3\frac{1}{2} + 2\frac{7}{9} =$

(e) $2\frac{3}{10} + 2\frac{1}{6} =$

(f) $2\frac{5}{6} + 2\frac{9}{10} =$

EXERCISE 6

1. Subtract. Write each answer in its simplest form.

(a) $3\frac{7}{8} - 1\frac{1}{2} = 2\frac{7}{8} - \frac{1}{2}$

$= 2\frac{7}{8} - \frac{\Box}{8}$

$=$

(b) $5\frac{4}{5} - 2\frac{1}{10} = 3\frac{4}{5} - \frac{1}{10}$

$= 3\frac{\Box}{10} - \frac{\Box}{10}$

$=$

(c) $4\frac{5}{6} - 2\frac{7}{12} =$

(d) $5\frac{11}{12} - 1\frac{3}{4} =$

(e) $4\frac{1}{9} - 2\frac{2}{3} =$

(f) $4\frac{1}{4} - 1\frac{5}{12} =$

2. Subtract. Write each answer in its simplest form.

(a) $4\frac{1}{2} - 1\frac{2}{9} = 3\frac{1}{2} - \frac{2}{9}$

$= 3\frac{\square}{18} - \frac{\square}{18}$

$=$

(b) $3\frac{3}{4} - 1\frac{2}{3} = 2\frac{3}{4} - \frac{2}{3}$

$= 2\frac{\square}{12} - \frac{\square}{12}$

$=$

(c) $3\frac{5}{9} - 1\frac{1}{2} =$

(d) $4\frac{7}{8} - 2\frac{5}{12} =$

(e) $4\frac{1}{4} - 2\frac{5}{6} =$

(f) $4\frac{3}{10} - 3\frac{5}{6} =$

EXERCISE 7

1. Add or subtract. Write each answer in its simplest form.

(a) $\frac{1}{6} + \frac{3}{10} =$	(b) $\frac{2}{3} + \frac{1}{12} =$	(c) $\frac{5}{12} + \frac{1}{8} =$
(d) $1\frac{3}{8} - \frac{7}{12} =$	(e) $1\frac{1}{3} - \frac{7}{10} =$	(f) $1\frac{3}{10} - \frac{5}{6} =$
(g) $3\frac{2}{9} + 1\frac{1}{6} =$	(h) $2\frac{5}{6} + 5\frac{1}{2} =$	(i) $2\frac{5}{6} + 1\frac{3}{8} =$
(j) $4\frac{1}{6} - 1\frac{2}{3} =$	(k) $3\frac{1}{6} - 2\frac{1}{10} =$	(l) $3\frac{3}{10} - 1\frac{1}{6} =$

2. Linda mowed $\frac{2}{5}$ of a lawn. Her brother mowed another $\frac{1}{4}$ of it. What fraction of the lawn did they mow?

---

3. Mary ate $\frac{1}{8}$ of a cake. Peter ate another $\frac{1}{4}$ of it.
   (a) What fraction of the cake did they eat altogether?
   (b) What fraction of the cake did Peter eat more than Mary?

---

4. Robert jogged $1\frac{2}{5}$ km. His brother jogged $2\frac{1}{2}$ km. Who jogged the longer distance? How much longer?

5. A container has a capacity of 3 L. It contains $1\frac{3}{4}$ L of water. How much more water is needed to fill the container completely?

---

6. Mr. Williams planned to spend $1\frac{1}{2}$ h to cook a meal. He finished the cooking in $1\frac{1}{12}$ h instead. How much earlier did he finish the cooking?

---

7. The total length of two ribbons is $2\frac{3}{4}$ m. If one ribbon is $1\frac{1}{3}$ m long, what is the length of the other ribbon?

EXERCISE 8

1. Multiply. Write the answer in its simplest form.

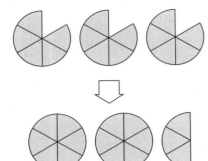

$\frac{5}{6} \times 3 =$ [ ]

2. Multiply $\frac{4}{5}$ and 3.

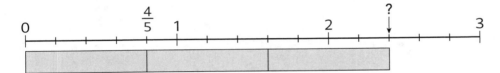

$\frac{4}{5} \times 3 =$ [ ]

3. Multiply 5 and $\frac{3}{4}$.

$5 \times \frac{3}{4} =$ [ ]

4. Multiply. Write each answer in its simplest form.

(a) $\frac{2}{5} \times 10 =$	(b) $\frac{1}{5} \times 6 =$	(c) $\frac{3}{5} \times 6 =$
(d) $5 \times \frac{1}{6} =$	(e) $5 \times \frac{5}{6} =$	(f) $10 \times \frac{5}{6} =$
(g) $\frac{3}{5} \times 4 =$	(h) $\frac{1}{4} \times 25 =$	(i) $4 \times \frac{2}{9} =$

EXERCISE 9

1. Find the value of each of the following.

(a)

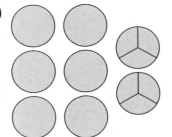 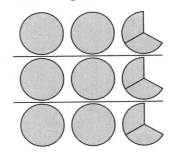

$\frac{1}{3}$ of 8 = ☐

(b)

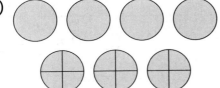 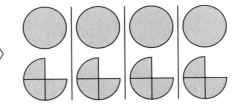

$\frac{1}{4}$ of 7 = ☐

(c)

 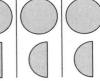

$\frac{5}{6}$ of 9 = ☐

(d)

$\frac{3}{8}$ of 10 = ☐

2. Find the value of each of the following.

(a) $\frac{1}{2}$ of $7 = \frac{1}{2} \times 7$ $=$	(b) $\frac{1}{3}$ of $10 =$
(c) $\frac{1}{4}$ of $5 =$	(d) $\frac{1}{5}$ of $9 =$
(e) $\frac{1}{4}$ of $2 =$	(f) $\frac{1}{6}$ of $10 =$
(g) $\frac{1}{8}$ of $20 =$	(h) $\frac{1}{10}$ of $25 =$

3. Find the value of each of the following.

(a) $\frac{2}{3}$ of $7 = \frac{2}{3} \times 7$ $=$	(b) $\frac{3}{5}$ of $6 =$
(c) $\frac{5}{6}$ of $5 =$	(d) $\frac{5}{8}$ of $9 =$
(e) $\frac{5}{9}$ of $3 =$	(f) $\frac{3}{10}$ of $8 =$
(g) $\frac{5}{6}$ of $10 =$	(h) $\frac{7}{8}$ of $20 =$

EXERCISE 10

1. Use the grid to draw a rectangle that is 4 in. by $3\frac{3}{4}$ in.

   Then find the area of the rectangle.

   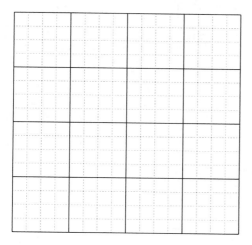

   Area = [   ] in.²

Find the value of each of the following.

2. $12 \times 4\frac{5}{8} = 12 \times 4 + 12 \times \dfrac{\square}{8}$

   $\phantom{12 \times 4\frac{5}{8}} = 48 + \dfrac{\square}{8}$

   $\phantom{12 \times 4\frac{5}{8}} = \boxed{}$

3. $7 \times 2\frac{4}{5} = 7 \times \dfrac{\square}{5}$

   $\phantom{7 \times 2\frac{4}{5}} = \dfrac{\square}{5}$

   $\phantom{7 \times 2\frac{4}{5}} = \boxed{}$

4. Multiply. Write each answer in its simplest form.

(a) $3\frac{2}{5} \times 6 =$

(b) $8\frac{1}{2} \times 13 =$

(c) $2\frac{3}{4} \times 25 =$

(d) $5 \times 3\frac{5}{12} =$

(e) $12 \times 4\frac{7}{10} =$

(f) $6\frac{1}{4} \times 100 =$

EXERCISE 11

1. There are 50 oranges in a box. Of them, $\frac{3}{10}$ are rotten.

    How many oranges are *not* rotten?

    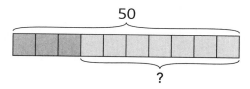

2. Petrina spent $\frac{2}{5}$ of her money and had $60 left.

    How much money did she have at first?

    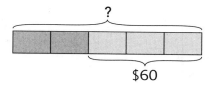

3. After spending \$30 on a shirt, Mark had $\frac{3}{8}$ of his money left. How much money did he have at first?

---

4. Of a group of children, $\frac{4}{7}$ are boys. If there are 18 more boys than girls, how many children are there altogether?

5. A tank is $\frac{4}{5}$ full of water. If 40 gal more water is needed to fill the tank completely, find the capacity of the tank.

6. There are 1,400 students in a school, of whom $\frac{1}{4}$ wear eyeglasses. Of those who wear eyeglasses, $\frac{2}{7}$ are boys. How many boys in the school wear eyeglasses?

7. Mrs. Ricci spent $\frac{1}{2}$ of her money on a camera and another $\frac{1}{8}$ on a radio. The camera costs $120 more than the radio. How much money did she have at first?

8. Larry had $480. He used $\frac{2}{3}$ of it to buy an electric fan. He also bought a tea set for $60. How much money did he have left?

9. After spending $\frac{2}{5}$ of her money on a video game, Sarah had $42 left. How much money did she have at first?

10. Find the area of a rectangle that measures $\frac{4}{5}$ yd by 6 yd.

11. Charles is making a patchwork quilt. Each quilt piece is a square with sides $1\frac{3}{4}$ ft. The quilt is 8 pieces long and 6 pieces wide.
    (a) How long is the quilt?
    (b) How wide is the quilt?

REVIEW 3

1. The figure is made up of identical rectangles. What fraction of the figure is shaded?

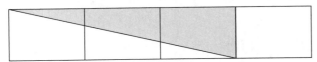

2. What is the missing number in the box?

$$\frac{13}{5} = 2 + \frac{\square}{5}$$

3. Find the value of each of the following.

   (a) $2\frac{3}{8} + \frac{7}{12}$

   (b) $4\frac{1}{3} - 1\frac{8}{9}$

   (c) $1\frac{3}{5} + 4\frac{3}{8}$

4. (a) Which one of the following is nearest to 4?

   $3\frac{1}{8}, \ 3\frac{11}{12}, \ 4\frac{9}{10}, \ 4\frac{4}{5}$

   (b) Which one of the following is greater than 2 but less than 3?

   $\frac{10}{3}, \ \frac{9}{5}, \ \frac{11}{4}, \ \frac{6}{2}$

5. (a) Write $8 \div 18$ as a fraction in its simplest form.

   (b) Write $\frac{46}{12}$ as a mixed number in its simplest form.

6. Write >, <, or = in each ◯.

(a) $4\frac{1}{2}$ ◯ $\frac{42}{4}$

(b) $3\frac{1}{7}$ ◯ $\frac{31}{7}$

(c) $\frac{34}{8}$ ◯ $4\frac{1}{4}$

(d) $10\frac{1}{3}$ ◯ $\frac{10}{3}$

7. What is the missing number in each of the following regular number patterns?

(a) $1\frac{1}{4}$, $1\frac{1}{2}$, $1\frac{3}{4}$, 2, ☐

(b) $4\frac{2}{3}$, $4\frac{1}{3}$, 4, ☐ , $3\frac{1}{3}$

8. (a) Arrange the fractions in decreasing order.

$\frac{9}{4}$, $2\frac{1}{12}$, $2\frac{1}{2}$, $\frac{12}{11}$

(b) Arrange the fractions in increasing order.

$\frac{3}{4}$, $\frac{3}{5}$, $\frac{5}{7}$

9. There are 35 children in a class.

Of them, $\frac{3}{5}$ can swim.

How many children cannot swim?

10. A farmer had 60 pineapples.

He sold $\frac{4}{5}$ of them at $3 each.

He sold the rest at 3 for $1.
How much money did he receive altogether?

11. What is the difference between 5 and $2\frac{1}{4}$?

12. A piece of wood is 5 ft long.

    Juan used $\frac{3}{4}$ of its length to make a shelf.

    What is the length in feet of the wood left?

    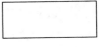

13. (a) How many months are there in $\frac{3}{8}$ of 2 years?

    (b) How many minutes are there in $\frac{5}{18}$ of 3 hours?

    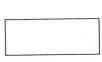

14. There are as many boys as girls in a class.

    If $\frac{2}{5}$ of the boys and $\frac{1}{2}$ of the girls go to

    school by bus, what fraction of the students
    in the class go to school by bus?

15. Mrs. Garcia had 6 lb of flour.

    She used $\frac{1}{5}$ of it to make bread.

    How many pounds of flour did she have left?

16. A ribbon is $\frac{3}{4}$ ft long. Express $\frac{3}{4}$ ft in inches.

17. Find the value of each of the following.

    (a) $5 \times 6\frac{3}{4}$

    (b) $15 \times 2\frac{1}{2}$

    (c) $1\frac{1}{3} \times 9$

18. A fish tank is $\frac{2}{5}$ full after Sara poured 14 gal of water

    into it. What is the capacity of the tank in gallons?

    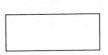

19. A group of children went swimming. Of them, $\frac{3}{8}$ were girls. If there were 40 boys, how many children were there altogether?

---

20. Taylor made $30 the first day selling magazines. The next day, she made $1\frac{4}{5}$ times as much as on the first day. How much money did she make on both days?

21. Jessica bought $\frac{3}{4}$ lb of berries. Mary bought $\frac{1}{6}$ lb of berries less than Jessica. What is the total weight of berries in pounds that they bought?

22. A container was $\frac{1}{2}$-filled with water. When 200 ml of water was poured out, it became $\frac{1}{3}$ full. Find the capacity of the container in milliliters.

EXERCISE 1

1. Find the value of each of the following.

(a)

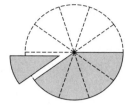

$$\frac{1}{5} \times \frac{1}{2} = \frac{1 \times 1}{5 \times 2}$$
$$=$$

$\frac{1}{5}$ of $\frac{1}{2} =$

(b)

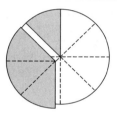

$$\frac{3}{4} \times \frac{1}{2} =$$

$\frac{3}{4}$ of $\frac{1}{2} =$

(c)

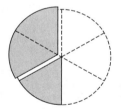

$$\frac{2}{3} \times \frac{1}{2} =$$

$\frac{2}{3}$ of $\frac{1}{2} =$

(d)

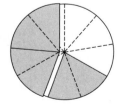

$$\frac{2}{3} \times \frac{2}{3} =$$

$\frac{2}{3}$ of $\frac{2}{3} =$

---

2. Mrs. Smith bought $\frac{5}{6}$ lb of meat. She cooked $\frac{2}{3}$ of it. How much meat did she cook?

$\frac{2}{3} \times \frac{5}{6} =$

3. A rectangle measures $\frac{3}{4}$ yd by $\frac{2}{5}$ yd. Find its area.

4. Susan spent $\frac{3}{5}$ of her money on a calculator and $\frac{2}{3}$ of the remainder on a pen. What fraction of her money did she have left?

EXERCISE 2

1. Multiply.

(a) $\dfrac{4}{9} \times \dfrac{1}{2} =$	(b) $\dfrac{1}{4} \times \dfrac{3}{8} =$
(c) $\dfrac{1}{5} \times \dfrac{3}{4} =$	(d) $\dfrac{5}{6} \times \dfrac{2}{3} =$
(e) $\dfrac{4}{5} \times \dfrac{5}{8} =$	(f) $\dfrac{4}{9} \times \dfrac{3}{10} =$
(g) $\dfrac{9}{10} \times \dfrac{5}{6} =$	(h) $\dfrac{3}{8} \times \dfrac{6}{7} =$

EXERCISE 3

1. Multiply.

(a) $2\frac{2}{3} \times 1\frac{2}{7} =$	(b) $7\frac{1}{5} \times 3\frac{5}{9} =$
(c) $3\frac{1}{2} \times 1\frac{6}{7} =$	(d) $4\frac{1}{2} \times 2\frac{2}{3} =$
(e) $8\frac{3}{4} \times 5\frac{5}{12} =$	(f) $6\frac{3}{10} \times 1\frac{7}{9} =$

2. Find the answers by following the arrows.

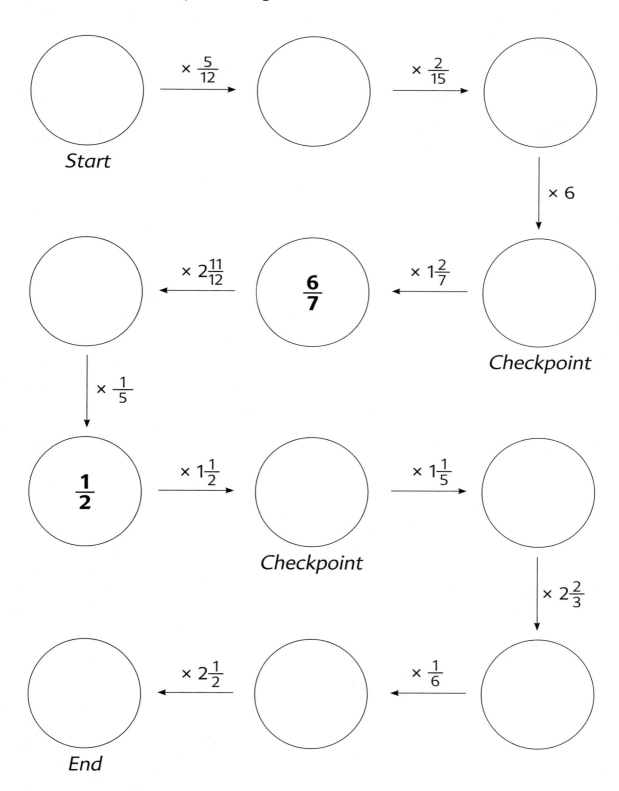

EXERCISE 4

1. Tracy bought 120 eggs. She fried $\frac{2}{3}$ of them and boiled $\frac{1}{4}$ of the remainder. How many eggs did she have left?

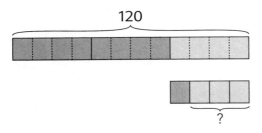

2. Mr. Ramirez had $600. He saved $\frac{3}{5}$ and spent $\frac{3}{8}$ of the remainder. How much did he spend?

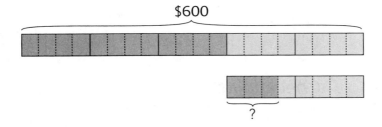

3. Lindsey made 400 tarts. She sold $\frac{3}{5}$ of them in the morning and $\frac{1}{4}$ of the remainder in the afternoon. How many tarts did she sell in the afternoon?

4. Mrs. Gray bought some eggs. She boiled $\frac{1}{2}$ of them and poached $\frac{1}{4}$ of the remainder. She had 9 eggs left. How many eggs did she buy?

5. Christina made some pancakes. She sold $\frac{3}{5}$ of them in the morning and $\frac{1}{4}$ of the remainder in the afternoon. If she had 300 pancakes left, how many pancakes did she make?

6. Mrs. Klein made some fruit buns. She sold $\frac{3}{5}$ of them in the morning and $\frac{1}{4}$ of the remainder in the afternoon. If she sold 200 more fruit buns in the morning than in the afternoon, how many fruit buns did she make?

7. Alex spent $\frac{1}{3}$ of his pocket money on a toy airplane and $\frac{2}{3}$ of the remainder on a toy robot. He had $20 left. How much did he spend altogether?

8. John spent $\frac{2}{3}$ of his money on a pen and a calculator. The calculator cost 3 times as much as the pen. If the calculator cost $24, how much money did he have left?

EXERCISE 5

1. Mrs. Ruiz bought $4\frac{4}{5}$ kg of beef. She cooked $\frac{3}{4}$ of it for dinner. How much beef did she cook?

2. Tess is sewing some quilts. She finished $2\frac{1}{2}$ quilts in the first month and $\frac{2}{3}$ of the remainder in the second month. She had $1\frac{1}{2}$ quilts left to sew in the third month. How many quilts did she sew in the 3 months?

Unit 4: Multiply and Divide Fractions

3. Carla has 6 large canning jars that each hold $1\frac{3}{5}$ L. She has made 10 L of applesauce. How much left over applesauce will there be when she has filled all the jars?

---

4. Rosa read 10 pages of a book on Monday. She read $\frac{1}{3}$ of the remainder on Tuesday. If she still had 24 pages to read, how many pages were there in the book?

5. Sam packed 42 kg of rice into one big bag and 6 small ones which were of the same size. The small bags each contained $\frac{1}{10}$ of the rice. How many kilograms of rice did the big bag contain?

6. Tyrone bought a bag of marbles. Of the marbles, $\frac{1}{4}$ were blue, $\frac{1}{8}$ were green and $\frac{1}{5}$ of the remainder were yellow marbles. If there were 24 yellow marbles, how many marbles did he buy?

7. After Paul hiked $\frac{5}{6}$ of a mile, he was $\frac{2}{3}$ of the way along the trail. How long is the trail?

8. Some students are waiting for buses to take them to a camp. There are enough students to fill $3\frac{3}{4}$ buses. Of the students, $\frac{2}{3}$ are girls. The boys are going to a different camp than the girls. How many buses are needed for just the girls?

EXERCISE 6

1. Find the value of each of the following.

(a) $\frac{1}{4} \div 2 = \frac{1}{4} \times \frac{1}{2}$

$=$

$\frac{1}{2}$ of $\frac{1}{4} =$

(b) $\frac{1}{3} \div 4 = \frac{1}{3} \times \frac{1}{4}$

$=$

$\frac{1}{4}$ of $\frac{1}{3} =$

(c) $\frac{1}{3} \div 3 = \frac{1}{3} \times \frac{1}{3}$

$=$

$\frac{1}{3}$ of $\frac{1}{3} =$

(d) $\frac{1}{2} \div 8 = \frac{1}{2} \times \frac{1}{8}$

$=$

$\frac{1}{8}$ of $\frac{1}{2} =$

2. A string of length $\frac{1}{3}$ m is cut into 2 equal pieces.
   What is the length of each piece?

3. Mrs. Jones divided $\frac{1}{4}$ kg of grapes equally among 6 children.
   How many kilograms of grapes did each child receive?

4. Divide. Then write a word problem for each.
   (a) $\frac{1}{3} \div 3$

   (b) $\frac{1}{5} \div 4$

EXERCISE 7

1. Find the value of each of the following.

(a) $\frac{2}{3} \div 4 = \frac{2}{3} \times \frac{1}{4}$

$=$

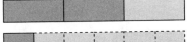

$\frac{1}{4}$ of $\frac{2}{3} =$

(b) $\frac{2}{3} \div 3 = \frac{2}{3} \times \frac{1}{3}$

$=$

$\frac{1}{3}$ of $\frac{2}{3} =$

(c) $\frac{4}{5} \div 8 = \frac{4}{5} \times \frac{1}{8}$

$=$

$\frac{1}{8}$ of $\frac{4}{5} =$

(d) $\frac{3}{4} \div 5 = \frac{3}{4} \times \frac{1}{5}$

$=$

$\frac{1}{5}$ of $\frac{3}{4} =$

Unit 4: Multiply and Divide Fractions

2. Divide.

(a) $\frac{3}{4} \div 2 =$	(b) $\frac{8}{9} \div 4 =$
(c) $\frac{5}{6} \div 5 =$	(d) $\frac{3}{5} \div 9 =$
(e) $\frac{4}{5} \div 2 =$	(f) $\frac{5}{7} \div 6 =$
(g) $\frac{5}{8} \div 3 =$	(h) $\frac{4}{9} \div 10 =$

3. Find the answers by following the arrows.

(a)

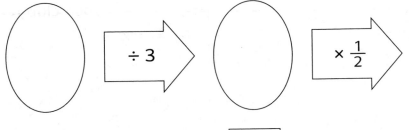

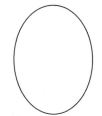 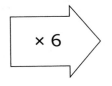 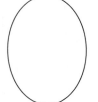 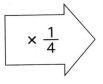 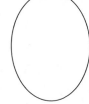

 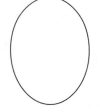 

(b)

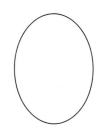 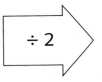 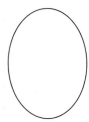 

Unit 4: Multiply and Divide Fractions

4. At a garage sale, $\frac{4}{5}$ of the money collected was divided equally among 4 clubs. What fraction of the money did each club receive?

5. Six cartons of drinks weigh $\frac{3}{10}$ kg. Find the weight of 1 carton of drink.

6. Sara poured $\frac{2}{5}$ pt of fruit juice equally into 4 cups. How much fruit juice was there in each cup?

7. The perimeter of a square is $\frac{3}{4}$ m. Find the length of each side in meters.

8. Mrs. Campbell used $\frac{3}{5}$ lb of sugar in 6 days. If she used the same amount each day, how much sugar did she use each day? Give your answer in pounds.

9. A pipe of length $\frac{1}{2}$ yd is cut into 5 equal pieces. What is the length of each piece in yards?

10. Mr. Knowles had a sum of money. He kept $\frac{1}{3}$ of it and divided the rest equally among his 4 children. What fraction of the sum of money did each of his children receive?

EXERCISE 8

1. Divide. Then use the pictures to check your answers.

(a)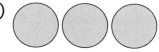

$3 \div \dfrac{1}{4} = 3 \times 4$

$\quad = $

3 wholes can be divided into _____ quarters.

(b)

$2 \div \dfrac{1}{5} = 2 \times$

$\quad = $

2 wholes can be divided into _____ fifths.

(c)

$4 \div \dfrac{1}{2} = 4 \times$

$\quad = $

4 wholes can be divided into _____ halves.

(d)

$3 \div \dfrac{1}{6} = 3 \times$

$\quad = $

3 wholes can be divided into _____ sixths.

---

2. Divide.

(a) $3 \div \frac{1}{2} = 3 \times 2$

$= $

(b) $3 \div \frac{1}{5} = 3 \times$

$= $

(c) $4 \div \frac{1}{3} =$

(d) $4 \div \frac{1}{4} =$

(e) $5 \div \frac{1}{5} =$

(f) $6 \div \frac{1}{3} =$

(g) $1 \div \frac{1}{8} =$

(h) $7 \div \frac{1}{6} =$

Unit 4: Multiply and Divide Fractions

3. How many $\frac{1}{2}$-hour periods will make up 4 hours?

---

4. How many pieces of string, each $\frac{1}{5}$ m long, can be cut from a string 3 m long?

---

5. A pail with a capacity of $\frac{1}{5}$ gal is used to add 4 gal of water to a tank. How many times must the pail be filled and poured into the tank?

EXERCISE 9

1. Divide.

(a) $\frac{1}{3} \div \frac{1}{3} =$	(b) $\frac{1}{2} \div \frac{1}{6} =$
(c) $\frac{1}{6} \div \frac{1}{4} =$	(d) $\frac{4}{5} \div \frac{1}{2} =$
(e) $\frac{2}{4} \div \frac{1}{4} =$	(f) $\frac{8}{9} \div \frac{1}{4} =$
(g) $\frac{3}{4} \div \frac{1}{2} =$	(h) $\frac{2}{3} \div \frac{1}{6} =$

Unit 4: Multiply and Divide Fractions

EXERCISE 10

1. Divide.

(a) $3 \div \frac{3}{4} =$	(b) $12 \div \frac{3}{4} =$
(c) $10 \div \frac{5}{8} =$	(d) $15 \div \frac{3}{5} =$
(e) $4 \div \frac{4}{5} =$	(f) $6 \div \frac{3}{4} =$
(g) $8 \div \frac{4}{5} =$	(h) $9 \div \frac{3}{8} =$

EXERCISE 11

1. Divide.

(a) $\frac{1}{2} \div \frac{2}{3} =$	(b) $\frac{2}{3} \div \frac{5}{6} =$
(c) $\frac{1}{8} \div \frac{3}{4} =$	(d) $\frac{4}{9} \div \frac{2}{3} =$
(e) $\frac{2}{5} \div \frac{3}{10} =$	(f) $\frac{2}{7} \div \frac{3}{5} =$
(g) $\frac{3}{8} \div \frac{3}{4} =$	(h) $\frac{5}{9} \div \frac{2}{3} =$

EXERCISE 12

1. A shopkeeper had 150 lb of rice. He sold $\frac{2}{5}$ of it and packed the remainder equally into 5 bags. Find the weight of the rice in each bag.

2. Peter had 400 stamps. Of them, $\frac{5}{8}$ are US stamps and the rest are Canadian stamps. He gave $\frac{1}{5}$ of the US stamps to his friend. How many stamps did he have left?

3. Kyle spent $\frac{2}{7}$ of his money on a gift for his wife and $\frac{3}{5}$ of the remainder on a new oven. If he had $300 left, how much money did he have at first?

---

4. In a box, $\frac{2}{3}$ of the beads are red, $\frac{1}{4}$ are yellow and the rest are blue. There are 42 more red beads than blue beads. How many beads are there altogether?

Unit 4: Multiply and Divide Fractions

5. There are 300 passengers on board an airplane. Of them, $\frac{2}{3}$ are men, $\frac{1}{4}$ are women and the rest are children. How many children are there?

6. There are 350 members in a swimming club. Of them, $\frac{2}{7}$ are new members. Of the new members, $\frac{3}{10}$ are females. How many new female members are there?

7. Sally made 500 gingerbread men. She sold $\frac{3}{4}$ of them and gave away $\frac{2}{5}$ of the remainder. How many gingerbread men did she give away?

8. Mr. Jackson made some sandwiches for a party. Of them, $\frac{3}{5}$ were chicken sandwiches and the rest were tuna sandwiches. There were 240 tuna sandwiches. How many chicken sandwiches were there?

9. Cameron has 480 stamps. Of them, $\frac{5}{8}$ are US stamps and the rest are foreign stamps. How many more US stamps than foreign stamps does he have?

---

10. Taylor bought 24 lb of flour. She used $\frac{1}{3}$ of it to bake fruit pies and $\frac{1}{4}$ of the remainder to bake some bread. How many pounds of flour were left?

EXERCISE 13

1. Lucy spent $\frac{3}{5}$ of her money on a handbag. She spent the rest of the money on a dress and a belt. The handbag cost twice as much as the dress. The dress cost $20 more than the belt. How much money did she have at first?

2. Gary spent $48 on a watch. He spent $\frac{1}{3}$ of the remainder on a pen. If he still had $\frac{1}{2}$ of his money left, how much money did he have at first?

3. After spending $\frac{1}{3}$ of her money on a TV and $\frac{1}{4}$ of it on a game console, Cindy still had $600 left. How much money did she spend on the game console?

4. Lucy spent $\frac{3}{5}$ of her money on a purse. She spent the remainder on 3 T-shirts which cost $4 each. How much did the purse cost?

5. Mary spent $\frac{3}{4}$ of her money on a jacket. She spent $\frac{1}{4}$ of the remainder on a shirt. The jacket cost $33 more than the shirt. How much did the jacket cost?

6. Henry bought 280 red and blue paper cups. He used $\frac{1}{3}$ of the blue ones and $\frac{1}{2}$ of the red ones at a party. He had an equal number of blue cups and red cups left. How many cups did he use at the party?

7. Mary had flowers, of which $\frac{3}{5}$ were roses and the rest were orchids. She sold $\frac{1}{2}$ of the roses and $\frac{1}{4}$ of the orchids. She then had 54 roses and orchids left. How many flowers did she have at first?

8. Andy spent $\frac{1}{3}$ of his money on some pastries and $\frac{3}{4}$ of his remaining money on 2 pies. Each pie cost 6 times as much as each pastry. If all the pastries cost the same, how many pastries did he buy?

REVIEW 4

1. Write each answer as a fraction or a mixed number in its simplest form.

(a) $\frac{3}{4} \times 15 =$	(b) $\frac{2}{5} \times \frac{5}{6} =$
(c) $\frac{8}{9} - \frac{3}{4} =$	(d) $\frac{6}{7} \div 4 =$
(e) $1\frac{4}{7} + 6\frac{1}{3} =$	(f) $\frac{4}{5} \div \frac{3}{6} =$

2. Find the value of each of the following.

(a) $\frac{2}{7} \times \frac{5}{8} =$	(b) $\frac{5}{6} \div \frac{1}{3} =$

3. What is the missing number in each box?

(a) $\frac{13}{5} = 2 + \frac{\boxed{}}{5}$

(b) $4\frac{1}{3} = \boxed{} \times \frac{1}{2}$

(c) $\frac{3}{5} \div \frac{1}{\boxed{}} = 3$

(d) $\frac{2}{3} \times \boxed{} = 16$

4. Find the value of each of the following.

   (a) $\frac{7}{9} \times \frac{3}{4}$

   (b) $36 \times \frac{5}{9}$

   (c) $\frac{2}{3} \div \frac{5}{6}$

   (d) $3 \div \frac{1}{8}$

5. Find the value of each of the following.

   (a) Divide $\frac{4}{9}$ by 6.

   (b) Multiply $\frac{4}{9}$ by 6.

   (c) Find the product of $\frac{4}{5}$ and $\frac{5}{8}$.

6. Fill in the missing number.

   (a) $\frac{1}{8} \times 3 + \frac{1}{8} + \frac{1}{8} + \frac{1}{8} = \frac{1}{8} \times$ [ ]

   (b) [ ] $\times \frac{3}{4} = 3$

7. Find the value of each of the following.

   (a) $2\frac{1}{2} \times (4 + \frac{11}{5})$

   (b) $6\frac{2}{3} - 2 \div \frac{1}{3} + \frac{3}{8}$

   (c) $\frac{1}{2} \div 3 + 5 \times 3\frac{3}{5}$

   (d) $[(\frac{1}{2} + \frac{3}{4}) \div \frac{1}{4}] \times 10^2$

8. If 100 g of prawns cost $2, find the cost of $\frac{1}{2}$ kg of prawns.

9. A piece of ribbon $\frac{2}{5}$ m long is cut into 4 equal pieces. Find the length of each piece in meters.

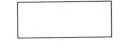

10. In a box, $\frac{1}{4}$ of the beads are red, $\frac{3}{5}$ of the remainder are yellow, and the rest are blue. If there are 48 blue beads, how many beads are there altogether?

11. Eight boxes of fudge weigh $\frac{2}{5}$ lb altogether. How many pounds do 5 boxes of fudge weigh?

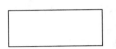

12. Each child ate $\frac{1}{6}$ of a pizza. How many children could eat a total of 4 pizzas?

13. A jug has $1\frac{2}{9}$ L of juice. All of it was poured equally into some glasses. Each glass had $\frac{1}{9}$ L of juice. How many glasses could be filled with the juice?

14. Jessica spent $\frac{1}{5}$ of her salary on rent and spent $\frac{1}{2}$ of the remainder on food. What fraction of her salary did she spend on food?

15. Six cups of water is $\frac{2}{3}$ of a jug. Find the total number of cups of water in the jug.

_____

16. Water is poured equally into 4 containers. Each container has 5 cups of water. How many quarts of water are there in the 4 containers?

_____

17. Brian bought 54 tangerines. He gave away $\frac{2}{3}$ of them and ate $\frac{1}{6}$ of the remainder. How many tangerines did he have left?

18. Mrs. Harris bought 4 lb of meat with $\frac{2}{5}$ of her money. She still had $24 left. How much did 1 lb of meat cost?

19. June spent $\frac{3}{5}$ of her money in the first week and $\frac{1}{3}$ of the remainder in the second week. She spent $110 altogether. How much money did she have left?

20. Marie read 42 pages of a book on Monday. She read $\frac{2}{5}$ of the book on Tuesday. If she still had $\frac{1}{4}$ of the book to read, how many pages were there in the book?

EXERCISE 1

1. Find the area of each figure. Then complete the table below.

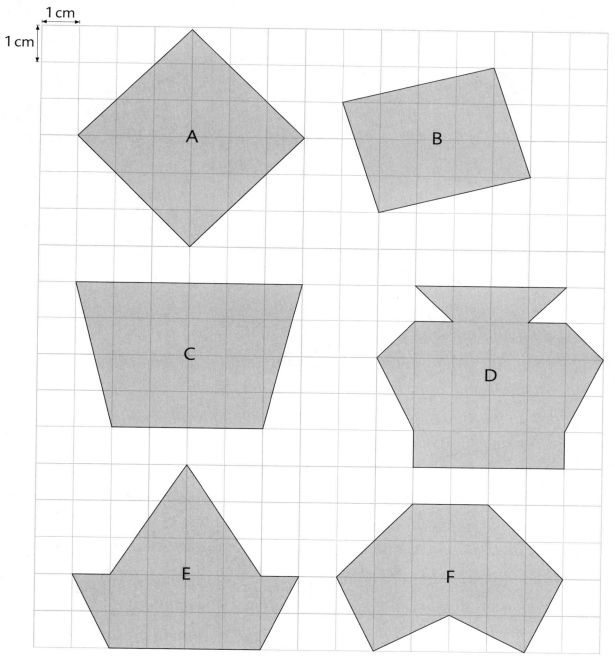

Figure	A	B	C	D	E	F
Area						

2. Find the area of each triangle. Then complete the table below.

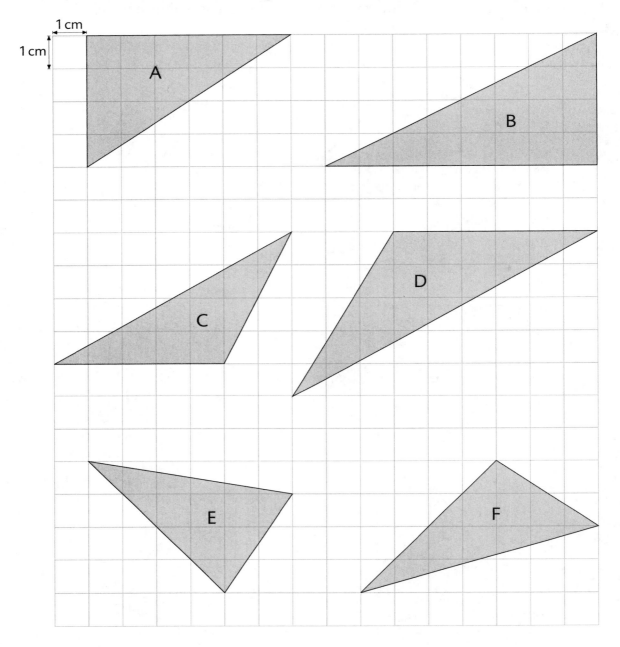

Figure	A	B	C	D	E	F
Area						

EXERCISE 2

1. Use the grid to make the rectangles given below. Find the area of each in square units. Write each answer in its simplest form.

   (a) 2 rows of 5 tiles, each $\frac{1}{2}$ unit by $\frac{1}{2}$ unit   Area = ☐

   (b) 4 rows of 9 tiles, each $\frac{1}{3}$ unit by $\frac{1}{6}$ unit   Area = ☐

   (c) 3 rows of 7 tiles, each $\frac{1}{4}$ unit by $\frac{1}{2}$ unit   Area = ☐

   (d) 5 rows of 6 tiles, each $1\frac{1}{4}$ unit by $\frac{1}{5}$ unit   Area = ☐

1 unit

1 unit

2. Find the area of each rectangle.

(a) 9 cm by 13 cm =

(b) $\frac{3}{4}$ m by 4 m =

(c) $\frac{5}{6}$ m by $\frac{3}{4}$ m =

(d) $5\frac{4}{9}$ cm by $\frac{3}{5}$ cm =

(e) $2\frac{1}{2}$ in. by $2\frac{3}{4}$ in. =

Unit 5: Perimeter and Area

EXERCISE 3

1. Find the area of each figure. Then complete the table below. (All the lines meet at right angles.)

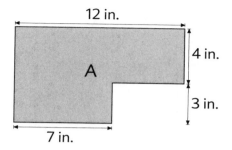

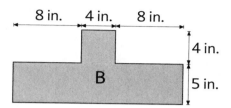

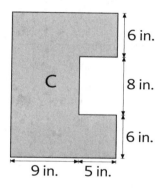

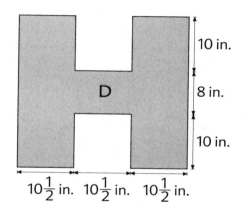

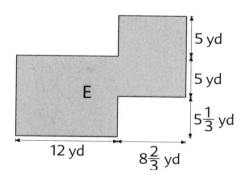

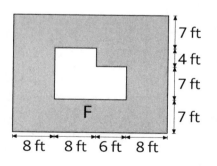

Figure	A	B	C	D	E	F
Area						

EXERCISE 4

1. Draw the height to the given base of each triangle.

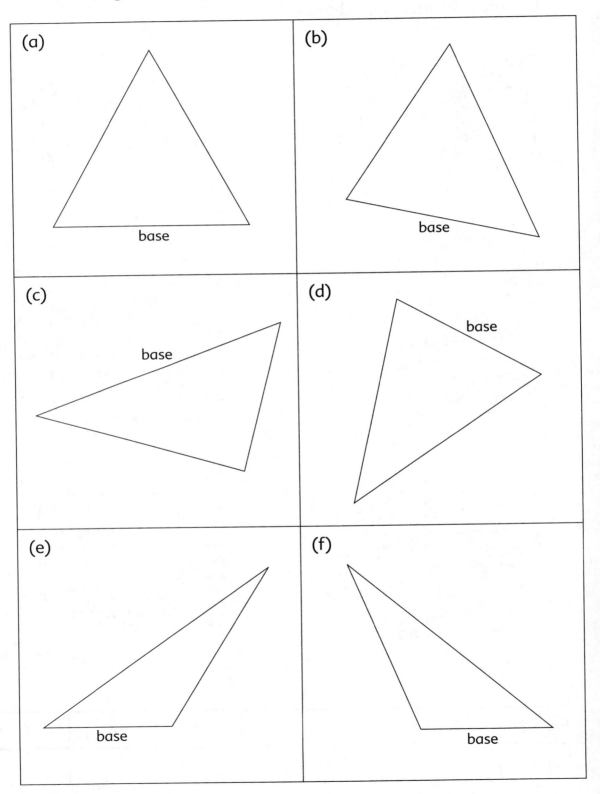

(a)

base

(b)

base

(c)

base

(d)

base

(e)

base

(f)

base

2. For each of the following triangles, name the base that is related to the given height.

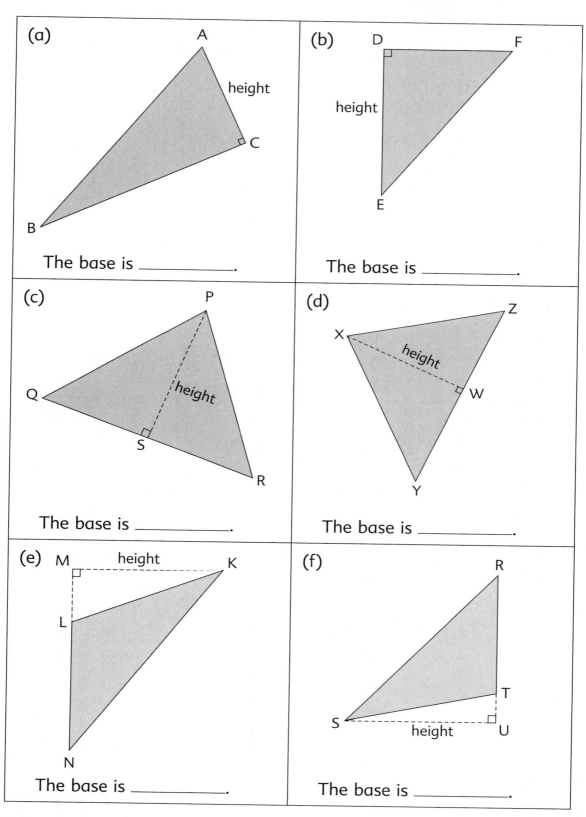

(a)

The base is _____.

(b)

The base is _____.

(c)

The base is _____.

(d)

The base is _____.

(e)

The base is _____.

(f)

The base is _____.

3. Find the area of each triangle.

(a)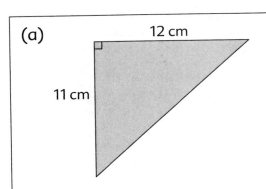
12 cm
11 cm

Area of the triangle

$= \frac{1}{2} \times 12$ cm $\times 11$ cm

$=$

(b)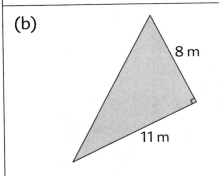
8 m
11 m

(c)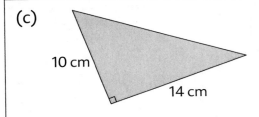
10 cm
14 cm

(d)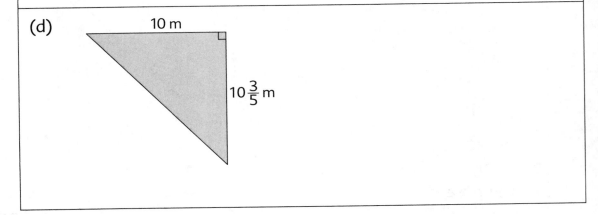
10 m
$10\frac{3}{5}$ m

Unit 5: Perimeter and Area

4. Find the area of each triangle.

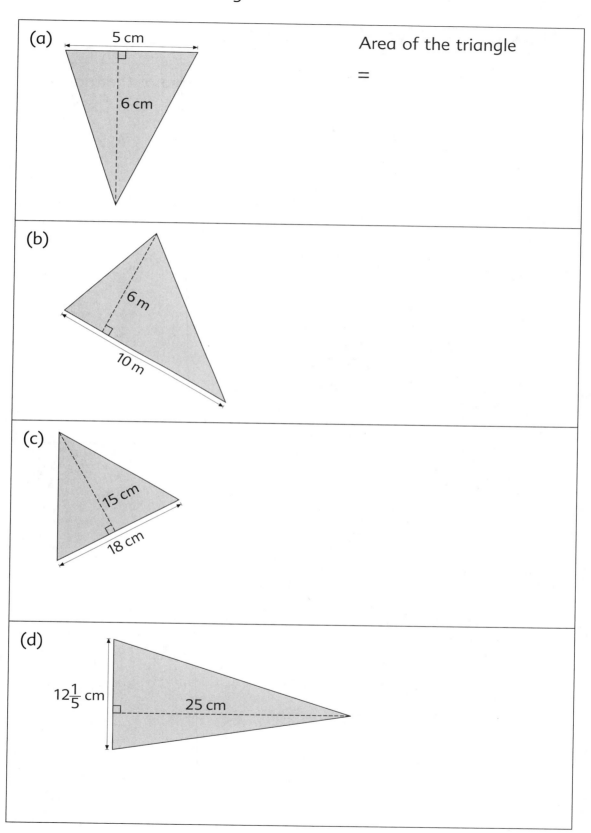

(a)   5 cm

6 cm

Area of the triangle

=

(b)

6 m

10 m

(c)

15 cm

18 cm

(d)

$12\frac{1}{5}$ cm   25 cm

EXERCISE 5

1. Find the area of each shaded triangle.

(a)

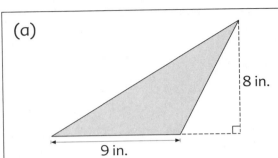

8 in.

9 in.

Area of the triangle

=

(b)

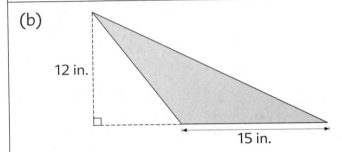

12 in.

15 in.

(c)

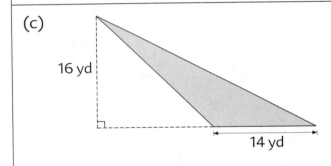

16 yd

14 yd

(d)

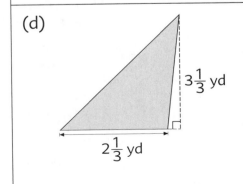

$3\frac{1}{3}$ yd

$2\frac{1}{3}$ yd

2. Find the area of each shaded triangle.

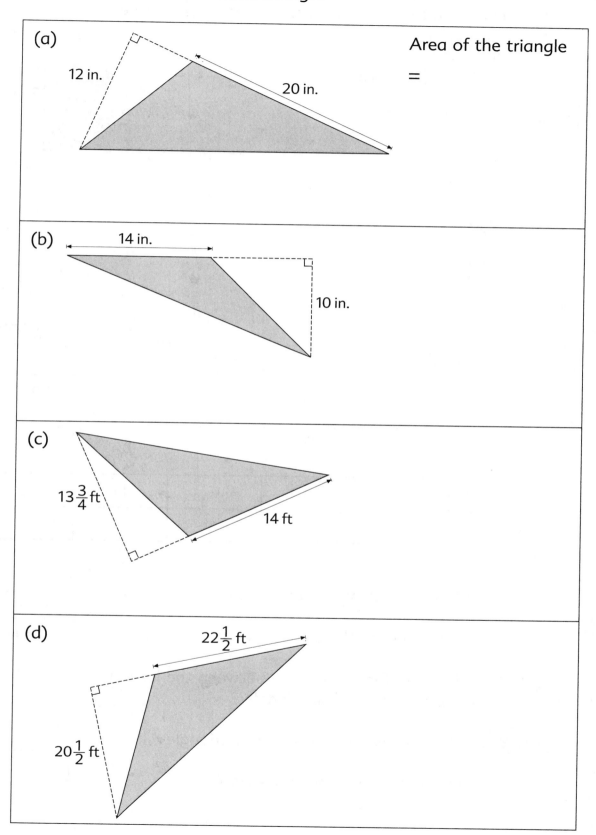

(a)

12 in.

20 in.

Area of the triangle

=

(b)

14 in.

10 in.

(c)

$13\frac{3}{4}$ ft

14 ft

(d)

$22\frac{1}{2}$ ft

$20\frac{1}{2}$ ft

3. Find the area of each shaded triangle.
   Then complete the table and answer the questions below.

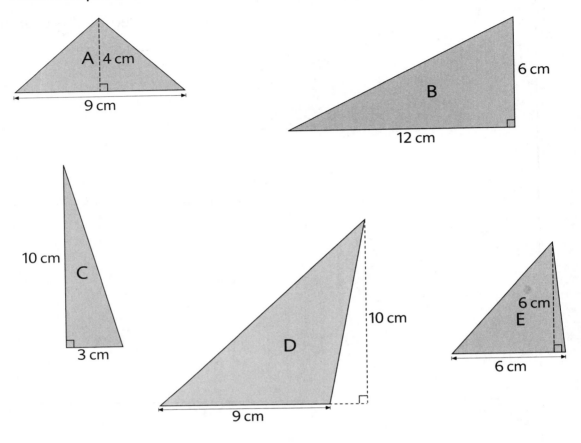

Triangle	A	B	C	D	E
Area					

(a) Which triangle has the largest area?

(b) Which triangle has the smallest area?

(c) What is the difference in area between the largest
    triangle and the smallest triangle?

(d) Which triangle is twice as large as Triangle A?

(e) Which triangles have the same area?

Unit 5: Perimeter and Area

EXERCISE 6

1. Find the area of each shaded triangle.

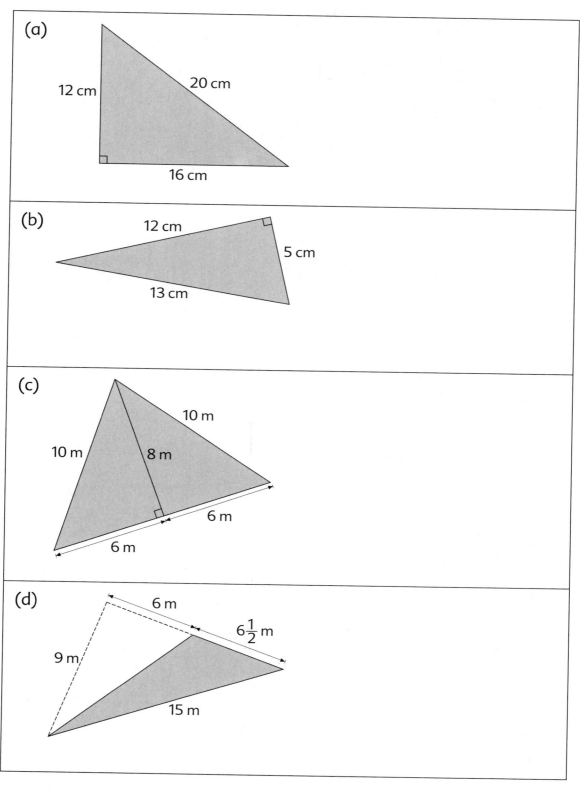

(a)

12 cm
20 cm
16 cm

(b)

12 cm
5 cm
13 cm

(c)

10 m
10 m
8 m
6 m
6 m

(d)

6 m
$6\frac{1}{2}$ m
9 m
15 m

2. Find the shaded area in each rectangle.

(a)

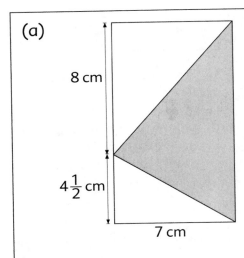

8 cm

$4\frac{1}{2}$ cm

7 cm

(b)

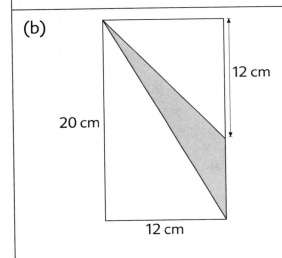

12 cm

20 cm

12 cm

Unit 5: Perimeter and Area

(c)

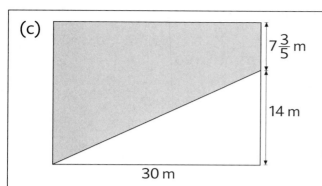

$7\frac{3}{5}$ m

14 m

30 m

(d)

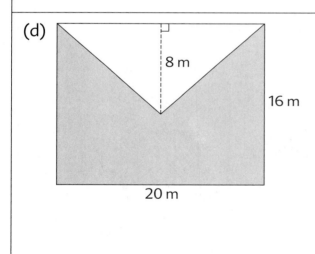

8 m

16 m

20 m

EXERCISE 7

1. Draw a different polygon with the same area.

(a)

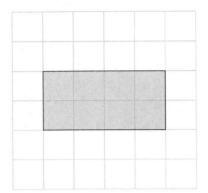 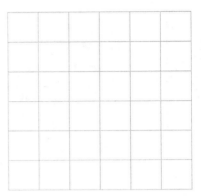

(b)

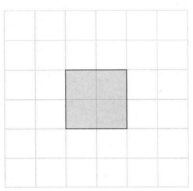 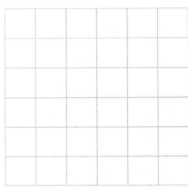

(c)

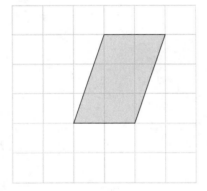 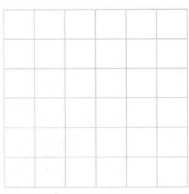

(d)

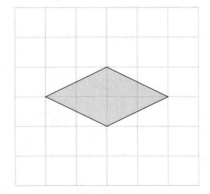 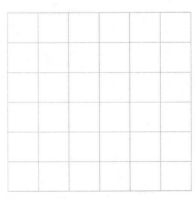

Unit 5: Perimeter and Area

2. Find the area of each figure.

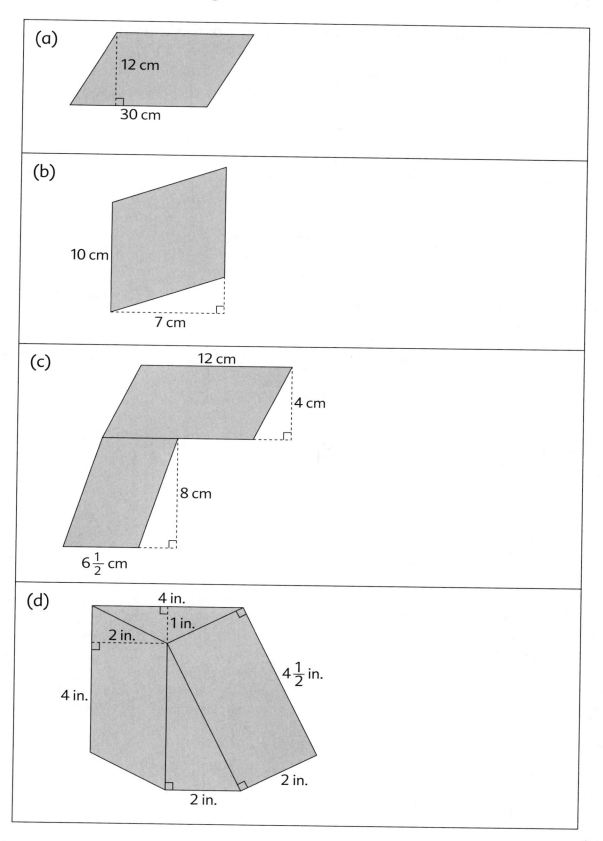

(a)

12 cm

30 cm

(b)

10 cm

7 cm

(c)

12 cm

4 cm

8 cm

$6\frac{1}{2}$ cm

(d)

4 in.

1 in.

2 in.

$4\frac{1}{2}$ in.

4 in.

2 in.

2 in.

REVIEW 5

1. (a) The figure is made up of a rectangle and a triangle. Find the area of the figure.

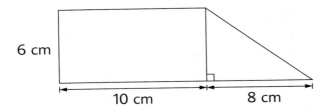

6 cm

10 cm   8 cm

(b) Find the area of the shaded triangle.

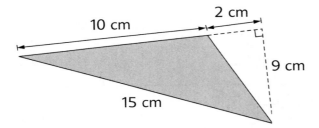

2 cm

10 cm

9 cm

15 cm

2. Find the area of each triangle.

(a)

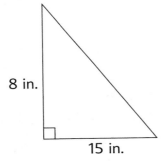

8 in.

15 in.

(b)

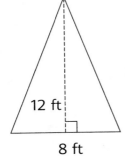

12 ft

8 ft

3. The figure is made up of 2-cm squares.

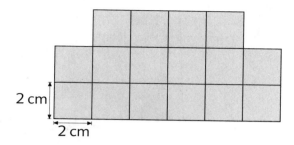

(a) Find the area of the figure.

(b) Find the perimeter of the figure.

4. (a) Draw a straight line to divide the figure into two parts of equal area.

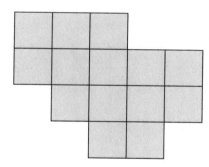

(b) The area of a square is 81 in.^{2}.
Find its perimeter.

5. Find the perimeter and area of each figure.
   (All the lines meet at right angles.)

(a)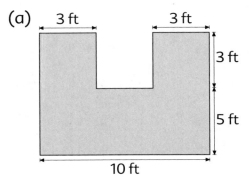

Area = [   ]

Perimeter = [   ]

(b)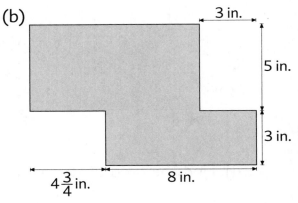

Area = [   ]

Perimeter = [   ]

6. Find the area of the figure.

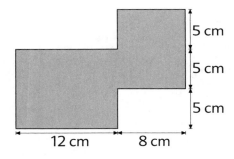

[   ]

7. The shaded figure is a parallelogram.
   Find the length of the side marked *a*.

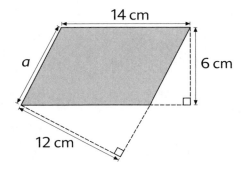

[   ]

8. This figure is made up of a square and two triangles. Find its area.

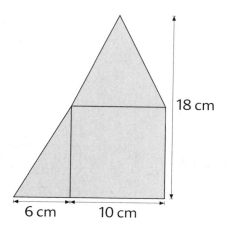

18 cm

6 cm   10 cm

9. Find the area and perimeter of the figure.

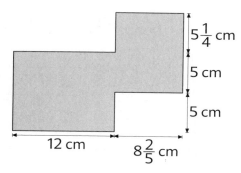

$5\frac{1}{4}$ cm

5 cm

5 cm

12 cm $8\frac{2}{5}$ cm

Perimeter =

Area =

10. The figure is made up of two parallelograms. Find its area.

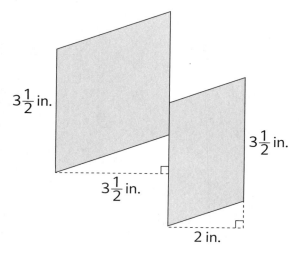

$3\frac{1}{2}$ in.

$3\frac{1}{2}$ in.

$3\frac{1}{2}$ in.

2 in.

11. The rectangle is made up of 6 unit squares. If the area of the rectangle is 54 cm², find its perimeter.

12. The perimeter of a square is 32 m.

    (a) Find the length of one side of the square.

    (b) Find its area.

13. The perimeter of a rectangle is 32 cm.
    If its width is 6 cm, find its length and area.

6 cm

?

Length =

Area =

14. The area of the shaded part is $\frac{1}{3}$ of the area of the rectangle. Find the area of the rectangle.

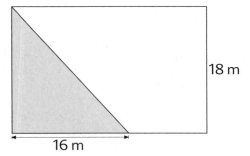

18 m

16 m

15. If the square has the same perimeter as the rectangle,
    find the area of the square.

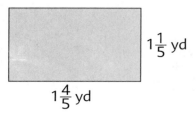 $1\frac{1}{5}$ yd

$1\frac{4}{5}$ yd

16. What fraction of the rectangle is shaded?

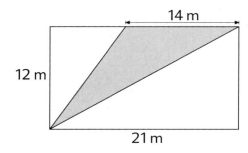

14 m

12 m

21 m

17. Find the shaded area in each of the rectangles.

   (a)

   10 in.

   $4\frac{3}{4}$ in.

   14 in.

   (b)

   3 ft

   12 ft

   5 ft   10 ft

18. The area of the square is the same as the area of the triangle. Find the perimeter of the square.

 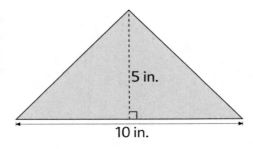

5 in.

10 in.

---

19. A rectangular piece of carpet is placed on the floor of a room leaving a margin of 1 yd around it. The room measures 7 yd by 6 yd. Find the cost of the carpet if 1 yd^2 of it costs $75.

EXERCISE 1

1.

   (a) The ratio of the number of tables to the number of chairs is

         [   ] : [   ] .

   (b) The ratio of the number of chairs to the number of tables is

         [   ] : [   ] .

2.

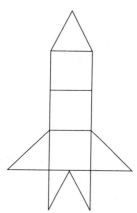

   (a) The ratio of the number of triangles to the number of squares is

         [   ] : [   ] .

   (b) The ratio of the number of squares to the number of triangles is

         [   ] : [   ] .

3.

   (a) The ratio of the number of circles to the number of triangles is

         [   ] : [   ] .

   (b) The ratio of the number of triangles to the number of squares is

         [   ] : [   ] .

4.

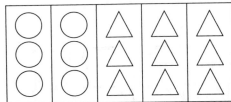

(a) The ratio of the number of circles to the number of triangles is

[   ] : [   ].

(b) The ratio of the number of triangles to the number of circles is

[   ] : [   ].

5.

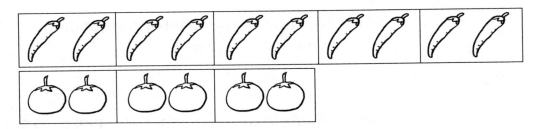

(a) The ratio of the number of peppers to the number of tomatoes is

[   ] : [   ].

(b) The ratio of the number of tomatoes to the number of peppers is

[   ] : [   ].

EXERCISE 2

1. Write each ratio in its simplest form.

   (a) John saves $12 and David saves $30.
       The ratio of John's savings to David's savings is

       [   ] : [   ] .

   (b) Mark bought 15 lb of rice and 9 lb of sugar.
       The ratio of the weight of sugar to the weight of rice is

       [   ] : [   ] .

2. Write each ratio in the simplest form.

6 : 9 = :	12 : 4 = :
6 : 24 = :	6 : 10 = :
25 : 15 = :	8 : 4 = :
15 : 18 = :	16 : 20 = :
20 : 40 = :	30 : 24 = :

3. Fill in the missing numbers.

   (a) 2 : 1 = 10 : [   ]   (b) 3 : 12 = [   ] : 4

   (c) 5 : 8 = 20 : [   ]   (d) 24 : 6 = [   ] : 3

   (e) 9 : 10 = [   ] : 40   (f) 2 : [   ] = 8 : 16

   (g) 4 : 5 = [   ] : 35   (h) 30 : [   ] = 6 : 3

   (i) 9 : 3 = 3 : [   ]   (j) [   ] : 5 = 5 : 25

   (k) 10 : 4 = 5 : [   ]   (l) [   ] : 3 = 24 : 18

4. The length of a rectangle is 60 in. and its width is 48 in. Find the ratio of the length to the width.

5. A ribbon 40 cm long is cut into two pieces. One piece is 16 cm long. Find the ratio of the length of the longer piece to the length of the shorter piece.

6. Peter saves $52. Sumin saves $20 more than Peter. Find the ratio of Peter's savings to Sumin's savings.

EXERCISE 3

1. The ratio of the number of apples to the number of oranges is 7 : 4. There are 60 oranges. How many apples are there?

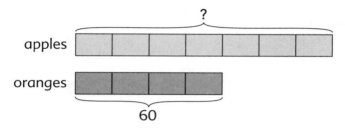

2. Sarah cuts a ribbon into two pieces in the ratio 5 : 3. The shorter piece is 42 cm long. What is the length of the original ribbon?

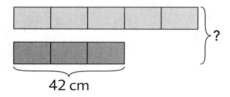

3. The ratio of the cost of a skirt to the cost of a blouse is 8 : 5. If the skirt costs $24 more than the blouse, find the cost of the blouse.

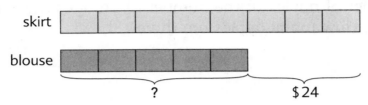

4. John and Peter shared $280 in the ratio 7 : 3. How much more money did John receive than Peter?

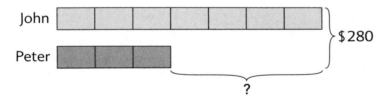

5. Ali won a cash prize of $50. He saved $35 and spent the rest. Find the ratio of the amount of money he saved to the amount of money he spent.

_____

6. In a swimming club, the ratio of the number of boys to the number of girls is 7 : 4. If there are 121 children in the swimming club, how many boys are there?

_____

7. Brianne made pineapple drinks by mixing pineapple syrup and water in the ratio 2 : 7. If she used 4 liters of pineapple syrup, how much water did she use?

EXERCISE 4

1.

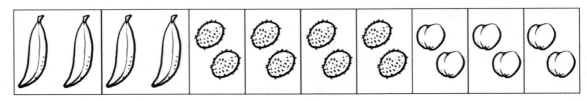

The ratio of the number of bananas to the number of kiwis to the number of apricots is [＿＿＿] : [＿＿＿] : [＿＿＿].

2.

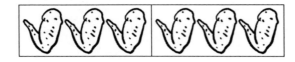

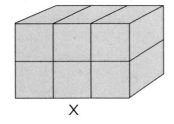

The ratio of the number of cupcakes to the number of chicken wings to the number of pastries is [＿＿＿] : [＿＿＿] : [＿＿＿].

3.

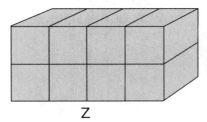

X   Y   Z

The ratio of the volume of Solid X to the volume of Solid Y to the volume of Solid Z is [＿＿＿] : [＿＿＿] : [＿＿＿].

4.

| Jim | Ravi | Tom |

Jim's weight : Ravi's weight : Tom's weight

= [   ] : [   ] : [   ]

5.

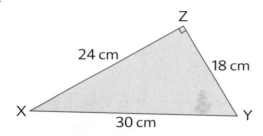

Length of XZ : Length of YZ : Length of XY

= [   ] : [   ] : [   ]

6. The table shows Mingli's savings for three months.

January	$12
February	$12
March	$8

Savings in January : Savings in February : Savings in March

= [   ] : [   ] : [   ]

EXERCISE 5

1. A box contains blue, green, and white beads. The ratio of the number of blue beads to the number of green beads to the number of white beads is 5 : 2 : 3. If there are 90 blue beads, how many beads are there altogether?

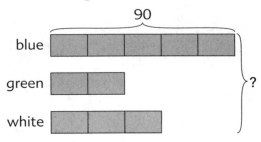

2. A piece of wire 45 cm long is bent to form a triangle. If the sides of the triangle are in the ratio 3 : 2 : 4, find the length of the longest side.

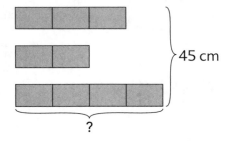

Unit 6: Ratio

3. The ratio of David's mass to Ryan's mass to Ali's mass is 8 : 5 : 4. If Ryan has a mass of 30 kg, find the total mass of the three boys.

4. Three boys share a sum of money in the ratio 5 : 3 : 2. If the smallest share is $30, find the biggest share.

REVIEW 6

1.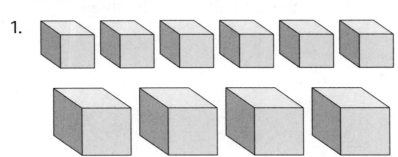

   (a) The ratio of the number of big cubes to the number of small cubes is [____] : [____].

   (b) The ratio of number of small cubes to the total number of cubes is [____] : [____].

2. Find the ratio of the length to the perimeter of the rectangle. Write the answer in its simplest form.

   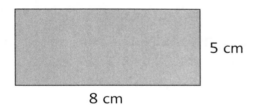

   5 cm

   8 cm

3. Alisha has 25 red beads and 15 blue beads. The ratio of number of red beads to number of blue beads is [____] : [____].

4. Fill in the missing numbers.

   (a) $3 : 8 =$ [____] $: 24$ (b) $5 : 6 : 3 = 25 :$ [____] $: 15$

   (c) $12 : 18 = 4 :$ [____]   (d) $9 : 27 = 3 :$ [____]

   (e) $7 : 3 =$ [____] $: 12$ (f) $4 :$ [____] $: 3 = 24 : 30 : 18$

5. Express each ratio in its simplest form.

(a) 20 : 12 = [ ]

(b) 18 : 21 = [ ]

(c) 48 : 36 = [ ]

(d) 42 : 12 = [ ]

(e) 18 : 30 : 72 = [ ]

6. The ratio of the number of books that Andy had to the number of books that Craig had was 1 : 2. After Andy bought 24 new books, the ratio became 2 : 1. How many books did Andy have at first?

7. What is the ratio of the area of the shaded part to the area of the unshaded part? Write the answer in its simplest form.

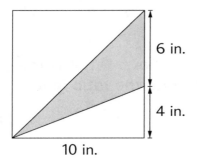

6 in.

4 in.

10 in.

8. The length and the width of a rectangle are in the ratio 5 : 3. The length of the rectangle is 20 in.

(a) Find its width.

(b) Find its area.

(c) Find its perimeter.

9. The sides of a triangle are in the ratio 5 : 2 : 4.
   The longest side of the triangle is 15 cm.

   (a) Find its shortest side.

   (b) Find its perimeter.

10. The ratio of the length of a rectangle to the width
    is 3 : 2. If the width is 9 cm, what is the area of
    the rectangle?

11. The ratio of Gary's mass to Andy's mass is 4 : 5.
    Their total mass is 117 kg.

    (a) Find Andy's mass.

    (b) Find Gary's mass.

12. The ratio of the height of a tree to the length of its
    shadow is 3 : 2. The height of the tree is 15 m.
    Find the length of its shadow.

13. There are 75 children in a lab. Of them, 45 are boys. What is the
    ratio of number of boys to number of girls? Write the ratio in its
    simplest form.

14. In a class there are 65 students. The ratio of the number of girls to the number of boys is 5 : 8. How many girls are there?

15. The ratio of Bill's money to Henry's money was 5 : 6. After Bill spent $800 on a TV set, the ratio became 1 : 2. How much money did Bill have at first?

16. Three boys, Juan, Seth, and Jared shared a number of stamps in the ratio 3 : 5 : 7. If Seth received 45 stamps, how many more stamps did Jared receive than Juan?

---

17. Mr. Jeff packed 150 apples into 3 boxes A, B, and C in the ratio of 5 : 2 : 3. Find the number of apples in Box C.

---

18. The ratio of money spent on a dress to the money spent on a scarf is 7 : 3. If the dress costs $36 more than the scarf, find the cost of the scarf.